THE
UNDERGROUND
RAILROAD

NAVIGATE THE JOURNEY
FROM SLAVERY TO FREEDOM

Judy Dodge Cummings
Illustrated by Tom Casteel

~ More American history titles in the *Build It Yourself* series ~

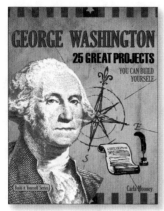
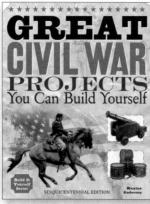
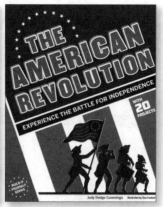
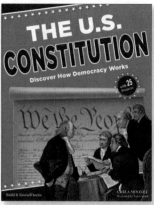

Check out more titles at www.nomadpress.net

Nomad Press
A division of Nomad Communications
10 9 8 7 6 5 4 3 2 1

This book was manufactured by Marquis Book Printing,
Montmagny, Québec, Canada
February 2017, Job #134265
ISBN Softcover: 978-1-61930-490-1
ISBN Hardcover: 978-1-61930-486-4

Educational Consultant, Marla Conn

Questions regarding the ordering of this book should be addressed to
Nomad Press
2456 Christian St.
White River Junction, VT 05001
www.nomadpress.net

Printed in Canada.

CONTENTS

Glossary | Resources | Essential Questions | Index

PS

Interested in Primary Sources?

Look for this icon. Use a smartphone or tablet app to scan the QR code and explore more! You can find a list of URLs on the Resources page. If the QR code doesn't work, try searching the Internet with the Keyword Prompts to find other helpful sources.

the Underground Railroad 🔎

1442: The Portuguese bring 10 captives from Africa to Europe, beginning the transatlantic slave trade.

1619: The first African slaves arrive in the North American colonies.

1775: The first organization to aid fugitive slaves is formed in Philadelphia, Pennsylvania.

1777: Vermont is the first state to ban slavery.

1780: Pennsylvania becomes the first state to pass a gradual emancipation law.

1787: Slavery is protected within the United States Constitution.

1793: Congress passes the first federal Fugitive Slave Law, making it illegal to aid slaves fleeing from slavery.

1831: Editor William Lloyd Garrison calls for immediate emancipation in the first issue of *The Liberator*.

1808: The international slave trade is outlawed, but this causes the American domestic slave trade to grow.

1831: Nat Turner leads a slave revolt in Virginia during which 60 white people are massacred, leading to harsh reprisals against all black people.

1816: The American Colonization Society is founded with the goal of resettling former slaves in either Africa or Latin America.

1826: Levi Coffin moves to Fountain City, Indiana, and establishes a station on the Underground Railroad that will become one of the most important in the nation.

1822: John Rankin moves from Kentucky to Ripley, Ohio, and enlarges Underground Railroad operations already in existence there.

1833: England outlaws slavery in its colonies, including Canada.

1833: The American Anti-Slavery Society is formed in Philadelphia.

1835: The New York Committee of Vigilance is formed in Manhattan and becomes a model used by other Underground Railroad organizers.

1849: The Reverend William King founds a settlement for blacks in Buxton, Ontario.

1838: "Eliza," the woman who is the model for a character in *Uncle Tom's Cabin*, escapes to freedom through the Underground Railroad in Ripley, Ohio.

1838: Frederick Bailey escapes from slavery in Maryland and changes his name to Frederick Douglass.

1851: The Christiana Riot in Lancaster County, Pennsylvania, prevents slave catchers from capturing fugitives and results in the death of slaveholder Edward Gorsuch.

1849: Harriet Tubman escapes from slavery in Maryland.

1845: Captain Jonathan Walker is arrested for aiding fugitive slaves in Florida and his hand is branded.

1854: The Kansas-Nebraska Act is passed, allowing western territories to vote on whether they want to be free states or slave states. This leads to a mini civil war in Kansas.

1861: Eleven slave states secede from the United States, forming their own country called the Confederate States of America. This leads to the Civil War between the Confederacy of the South and the Union of the North, which lasts until 1865.

1865: The Civil War ends and the 13th Amendment to the Constitution is ratified, which abolishes slavery in the United States forever.

1859: John Brown tries to launch a slave revolt at Harper's Ferry, Virginia, but is captured, tried, and executed.

A HISTORIC SECRET

Can you keep a secret? What if it was a secret you could never tell because it was a matter of life and death? There was a secret in history that few people knew. Knowledge of this information was once so dangerous, so deadly, that only the strongest, bravest, and most reliable people could be trusted as secret keepers. Could you carry that kind of burden?

For more than two centuries in the United States, slavery was the law of the land. People could be bought and sold the way someone today might buy a house or a car or a cow. They were forced to work under brutal conditions for long hours and no pay. Who were these people? They were Africans who had been kidnapped from their homeland, transported to America, and sold on the **auction block**.

Decade after decade, slavery grew in the United States. By 1860, there were 4 million African Americans living in **bondage** in the United States.

WORDS TO KNOW

auction: a public sale of property to the highest bidder.

auction block: the platform from which an auctioneer sells goods to a crowd of buyers.

bondage: another word for slavery.

1

enslave: to make someone a slave.

fugitive: someone who runs away to avoid being captured.

abolitionist: someone who believed that slavery should be abolished, or ended.

abolish: to completely do away with something.

Underground Railroad: a system of cooperation among people who believed slavery was wrong that secretly helped fugitive slaves reach the Northern states and Canada.

Deep South: a region of the Southeastern United States that includes the states of Alabama, Georgia, Louisiana, Mississippi, North Carolina, and South Carolina.

legend: a story from the past that cannot be proved true.

network: a group of people who work together for a common cause.

Slaves had no rights. They could not go to school. Their owners could legally beat them for any reason or for no reason at all. Worst of all, families were often separated when fathers, mothers, or children were sold off, never to be seen again.

For many years, American society resisted granting slaves their freedom. During this time, some **enslaved** people ran away from their owners. Many of these **fugitives** were caught and returned to their owners and severely punished. However, some escaped and reached a free land. This is the secret part.

THE BEST-KEPT SECRET OF THE NINETEENTH CENTURY

A small group of free people called **abolitionists** hated slavery almost as much as the slaves did. They wanted to **abolish** slavery. Until that could happen, they created a crafty system called the **Underground Railroad** to help slaves escape. What the railroad was, how it worked, and who operated it was the best-kept secret of the nineteenth century.

When you read the phrase *Underground Railroad*, what do you imagine? Dark tunnels deep in the center of the earth? A train careening at top speed, its headlight illuminating the rocky belly of a mountain? Haunted faces peering out train windows?

That is a dramatic picture, but it's also a false one. The Underground Railroad was not underground and it was not a train. It was a process. Slaves ran away from their owners, most by fleeing north to free states or to Canada.

DID YOU KNOW?

Historians believe that about 100,000 people escaped from slavery on the Underground Railroad.

Free people, both black and white, helped the runaways by guiding them, hiding them, transporting them, and sometimes fighting for them. Because it was against the law to aid fugitives, sheriffs and slave catchers prowled back roads and city streets searching for runaways. Slaves who were caught were physically punished and brought back to the **Deep South**. Their helpers could be heavily fined and imprisoned.

To guard against this fate, the Underground Railroad was a tightly held secret.

Because the Underground Railroad was kept under wraps for so many years, rumors about the organization arose. People filled in missing facts with their imaginations. This was how the Underground Railroad was transformed from history to story.

Origin of the Name

How the Underground Railroad got its name remains a mystery, but **legend** suggests one origin. In 1831, a slave named Tice Davids swam across the Ohio River, vanishing on the other side. His owner told friends that Davids had disappeared on an "underground road." Historians cannot verify this account, but one fact is certain. By the 1840s, the term *Underground Railroad* was used by people across the country to refer to the escape **network**.

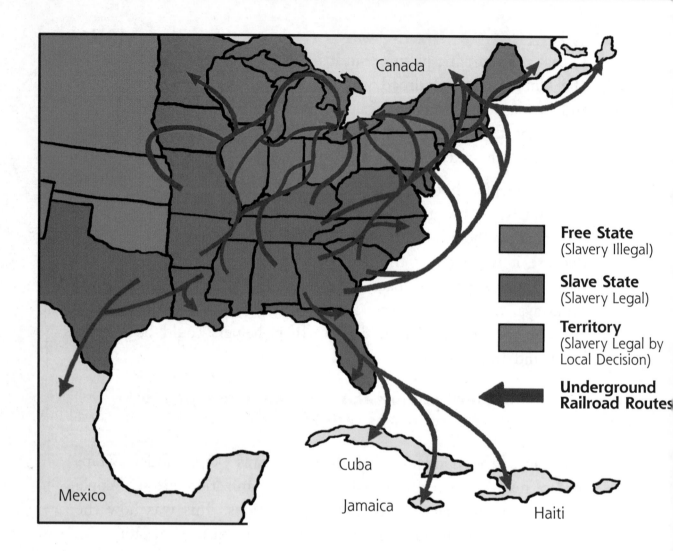

Free State (Slavery Illegal)

Slave State (Slavery Legal)

Territory (Slavery Legal by Local Decision)

Underground Railroad Routes

Canada

Mexico

Cuba

Jamaica

Haiti

Some people think of Harriet Tubman single-handedly leading hundreds of slaves to safety or courageous white conductors shepherding exhausted slaves from the Deep South all the way to Canada. Maybe they picture fugitives concealed in elaborate tunnels or slave quilts hanging from porch posts with hidden messages sewn into their patterns. Grains of truth are **embedded** in these legends, but much of what people believe about the Underground Railroad is not accurate or complete.

WORDS TO KNOW

embed: to put something firmly inside of something else.

resistance: a fight to prevent something from happening.

navigate: to find a way to get to a place when you are traveling.

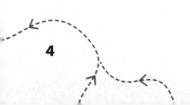

In this book, you will glimpse what life was like for enslaved people and how they fought the system that shackled them.

You will meet a few brave people and learn how their individual acts of courage evolved into the greatest campaign of **resistance** the nation has ever seen. You will trail fugitives as they **navigate** the wilderness to freedom—the final stop on the Underground Railroad.

Throughout the trip, you will have the opportunity to experience some of what nineteenth-century American life was like. You will examine the thinking of white Americans, some who supported slavery and others who wanted to destroy it forever. You will design wanted posters and memorials and navigate by the stars. You will use math and music and art to explore the impact the Underground Railroad had on American history.

Once you know the history of the Underground Railroad, your job is to spread the word. Gone are the days when knowing this information could get you killed. The Underground Railroad is no longer a secret. Now, it's part of history for all Americans.

Good Study Practices

Every good historian keeps a history journal! As you read through this book and do the activities, keep track of your ideas and observations and record them in your history journal.

Each chapter of this book begins with an essential question to help guide your exploration of the Underground Railroad. Keep the question in your mind as you read the chapter. At the end of each chapter, use your history journal to record your thoughts and answers.

? ESSENTIAL QUESTION

Why are there many myths and legends about the Underground Railroad?

Chapter 1

THE PECULIAR INSTITUTION

To understand the Underground Railroad, you first
need to learn about slavery. Slavery is deeply rooted
in human history—it began with the first **civilizations**.
Slavery in North America affected millions of people,
including a man named Josiah Henson and his family.

Josiah Henson was three years old when his father came home
with his ear cut off. Born in Maryland in 1789, Josiah was a
slave like his parents. An **overseer** had hurt Josiah's mother, so
his father attacked the man. The overseer tied Josiah's father to a
post, whipped him 100 times, and then
sliced his ear off. Josiah could hear his
father's screams from a mile off.

As final punishment, the slave was
sold. After that, Josiah never saw his
father again.

? ESSENTIAL QUESTION

How did the U.S.
Constitution enable
Southern states to maintain
the institution of slavery?

This event scarred Josiah. He vowed to be the perfect slave so his owner would never have an excuse to hurt him the way his father had been hurt. However, the institution of slavery did not play by **predictable** rules. While Josiah was everything his owner wanted—strong, obedient, and loyal—it was not enough. We'll learn more about the journey of Josiah and his family in the following chapters.

THE TRIANGULAR TRADE

The slavery that shaped the life of Josiah Henson and millions of other American slaves began with a trade network. This network was known as the **Triangular Trade**.

civilization: a community of people that is advanced in art, science, and government.

overseer: a person who supervises workers.

predictable: to know what will happen next.

Triangular Trade: a transatlantic trade network in which slaves and manufactured goods were exchanged between Africa, Europe, the Caribbean, and the American colonies.

status: the position or rank of one group in society compared to another group.

race: a group of people that shares distinct physical qualities, such as skin color.

WORDS TO KNOW

Slavery of a Different Sort

Slavery existed in Africa long before the first European set foot on the continent. African slavery was different from the system that developed in the United States. African slaves had the right to marry and own property. After working for a certain number of years, African slaves were set free. Slave **status** was not passed down from parents to their children and was not linked to skin color. In contrast, American slaves had no rights at all. Slavery was based on **race**, and if a child's mother was a slave, then that child was born a slave.

colony: an area that is controlled by or belongs to another country.

coffle: a line of slaves fastened together.

Middle Passage: the forced voyage of enslaved Africans across the Atlantic Ocean to the Americas.

contagion: the spreading of a disease.

transatlantic slave trade: the buying and selling of enslaved Africans to buyers in Europe and the Americas that lasted from the fifteenth through the nineteenth centuries.

WORDS TO KNOW

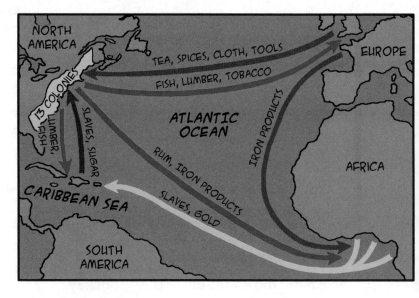

In this trade network, captured Africans and other goods were exchanged between Africa, Europe, the West Indies, and the American **colonies**. The system began in 1442, when Portuguese explorers returned from Africa with a cargo hold full of gold dust and 10 African slaves.

Once Portugal began to trade slaves, other European countries quickly joined in. Spain, France, the Netherlands, and Great Britain all bought African people to grow their sugar, cotton, coffee, and tobacco. Traders captured African men, women, and children from their villages and chained them together in long lines called **coffles**. The captives were marched to forts on the west coast of Africa and held in damp, dark dungeons for weeks or months until European merchants purchased them in exchange for rum, cloth, or guns.

The next phase of the captives' nightmare was called the "**Middle Passage**." On this leg of the Triangular Trade, captured Africans were transported across the Atlantic Ocean to the islands of the West Indies, where they were sold at auction. The voyage usually lasted two months.

Captives were confined below deck in a space the size of a coffin. Adults were crammed into bunks 16 inches wide, 32 inches high, and 5 feet, 11 inches long. Chains linked people together by the neck, leg, or arm. They could not easily reach the pots placed at the ends of the bunks to use as toilets, so they had to lie in their own waste for hours. Once a day, the crew brought the captives up on deck so the cargo hold could be rinsed out.

DID YOU KNOW? Slaves became so valuable that they were known as "black gold."

In conditions such as this, it is not surprising that disease jumped from person to person. Ship captains often ordered sick captives thrown overboard to try to stop the **contagion**, but smallpox and yellow fever killed many Africans.

During the course of the transatlantic slave trade, between 1 and 2 million people died on the Middle Passage.

SLAVERY IN THE AMERICAN COLONIES

In the late summer of 1619, a Dutch ship appeared in the Chesapeake Bay on the coast of Virginia. Settlers of Jamestown, the first British colony in North America, watched as the ship dropped anchor in their harbor. The ship's cargo was empty, except for 20 Africans that the Dutch crew had recently captured from a Spanish ship. The captain traded the captives for food and supplies.

WORDS TO KNOW

indentured servant: a person bound by contract to work a certain number of years without pay.

plantation: a large farm where one kind of crop is grown for export.

racism: negative opinions or treatment of people based on race.

inherited trait: a characteristic passed down from parent to child.

monitor: to watch or keep track of something or someone.

distinct: clearly different.

Slavery had arrived in America and soon spread to other colonies.

Not all people of color were considered slaves. Poor whites, blacks, and Native Americans also worked as **indentured servants**. These servants were bound by a contract to work for a certain number of years without pay. They received a place to live and food to eat, called room and board, and some training. After working out their contract, indentured servants were freed.

That freedom was a problem for rich, white **plantation** owners. Indentured servants were not a reliable class of workers because they eventually became free and moved on to other jobs. Plantation owners wanted a class of workers they could keep. They found a solution through **racism**.

By the end of the seventeenth century, the colonies had passed laws that said whites could work as indentured servants, but blacks were considered slaves for life. Bondage was linked to a permanent physical characteristic—skin color. To guarantee a steady supply of slaves, the colonies also declared that any children of an enslaved woman were also slaves. Slavery, like skin color, was now an **inherited trait**. After these laws were passed, slavery became embedded in American society.

DID YOU KNOW?

Follow the journey of four captured Africans as they are kidnapped and forced on board a slave ship in 1780. What challenges do these captives face? How are their experiences similar and how are they different?

PS

Liverpool slave stories

Slavery was legal in the Northern colonies, but not common. White people in the Northern colonies lived on small family farms. Slaves were expensive to buy and keep, and Northerners had no reason to own such costly property.

However, the Northern economy was part of the web of American slavery. New England workers built the ships that sailed to Africa to purchase slaves. Rum made in Northern distilleries was traded to African merchants in exchange for slaves.

Most enslaved people lived in the Southern colonies. Tobacco, rice, indigo, and cotton all grew in this warm climate, and these crops required a large labor force. On huge plantations, an overseer often **monitored** slaves in the field. At the end of the day, these workers returned to cabins, where they lived together. Living in groups allowed enslaved people to develop their own **distinct** culture and maintain traditions from Africa.

Slave huts (Library of Congress)

WORDS TO KNOW

delegate: a person sent to a meeting as a representative of a larger group of people or a specific area of the country.

ideal: a standard or belief that people strive to achieve.

WORDS TO KNOW

LIBERTY FOR SOME, NOT ALL

As colonists of Great Britain, Americans had to follow trade laws created by political leaders in London. Many Americans believed these regulations unfairly restricted their freedom. They felt like slaves, and they were sick of it. The colonists began to resist.

Tensions between colonists and Great Britain grew and reached a breaking point in 1776. American leaders who gathered in Philadelphia, Pennsylvania, decided the time had come to separate from the British Empire and form their own country. Virginian Thomas Jefferson drafted the Declaration of Independence. He wrote ". . . all men are created equal . . ." and all people had certain rights that no one, not even the government, could take away. These rights included ". . . life, liberty, and the pursuit of happiness." This document formed the foundation for the future government of the United States of America.

Some white Americans, including Jefferson himself, realized the colonists were demanding rights for themselves that they refused to give to others. While colonists demanded their own freedom from Britain, they continued to enslave African Americans. In his first draft of the Declaration, Jefferson wrote that slavery was against the "most sacred rights of life and liberty." However, **delegates** from South Carolina and Georgia demanded this clause be removed.

DID YOU KNOW?

The *São José Paquete de Africa* was a Portuguese slave ship that sank off the coast of South Africa in 1794. It was recovered in the 1980s. You can see some of the artifacts that were recovered from the ship at this website.

National Museum slave shipwreck found 🔍

Ready for Sale

Slave traders spent the summer months traveling around the South, buying slaves. Men, women, and children were housed in slave pens until they were sold at auction. Before the sale, the slaves were groomed. Gray hairs were plucked out or dyed to disguise slaves' ages. Slaves were fattened up on meat and butter. On the day of the auction, auctioneers ordered the captives to dance and jump about. Buyers felt each slave's muscles and looked at the slave's teeth so they could check the quality of the person they were purchasing.

A slave pen where slaves where kept before auction (Library of Congress)

The final version of the Declaration of Independence says nothing against the slave trade. Why do you think those states were concerned with that line?

The Revolutionary War between the American colonies and the British Empire had erupted in 1775. There were some African Americans who joined the colonists because they believed they had a better chance of freedom in a new nation founded on the **ideals** of the Declaration of Independence.

However, most blacks sided with the British. The British Army encouraged slaves to escape and join their army, promising them freedom when the war ended. Although the British only wanted men of fighting age, an estimated 100,000 slaves, males and females of all ages, fled to British lines.

emancipate: to legally free someone.

constitution: the basic principles and laws of a nation.

amendment: a correction, addition, or change to the U.S. Constitution.

congregation: the people who regularly attend a church.

The colonists won the war in 1783. The new nation of the United States of America had to create the structure of the government and legal system. Immediately, the founding fathers began to debate what role slavery would play in the new country.

POLITICAL COMPROMISES

Four years later, through the hot summer of 1787, political leaders debated what form the new government would take. Some Northern states had already passed laws that either abolished slavery or gradually **emancipated** slaves. However, only 40,000 slaves lived in the North. More than 650,000 lived in Southern states, and this population of slaves made up 60 percent of the South's wealth. Southerners had no intention of freeing their slaves. Like it or not, America was stuck with what some called the "peculiar institution."

The debate over slavery was fierce and the convention called to write the U.S. **Constitution** almost collapsed, but the leaders finally compromised. Southerners got some of what they wanted. Slavery remained legal and protected. Although slaves could not vote, each slave counted as three-fifths of a person when determining how many representatives a state had in the U.S. House of Representatives. This gave Southern states more voting power in the House. They also passed a fugitive slave law that permitted owners to pursue and recapture slaves who had run away to free states.

Supporters of slavery got the better deal, though Northern states did not walk away empty-handed. No new slaves could be imported from other countries after 1808, and slavery was banned in territories north of the Ohio River.

Although the word "slavery" never appeared in early drafts of or **amendments** to the Constitution, the Constitution was clear— the United States was a slave nation.

FREE NORTH AND SLAVE SOUTH

In the years following the Revolution, many people thought slavery would die a natural death. Some slaveholders wanted to create a nation based on the principle that all men were created equal, so they freed their slaves. Additionally, religious leaders in Quaker, Baptist, Methodist, and Presbyterian **congregations** preached that slaves were their brothers and sisters before God and should be free.

Between 1790 and 1810, hundreds of owners freed their slaves. Pennsylvania's slave population shrank from 8,887 to 4,177. In Delaware, the number of free blacks skyrocketed from 30 percent of the state's black population to 75 percent. Thomas Jefferson believed "The spirit of the master is abating . . . preparing for a total emancipation."

A technological breakthrough changed everything, though. A man named Eli Whitney (1765–1825) invented a cotton cleaning machine in 1793 called a cotton gin. By hand, it took a slave an entire day to clean one pound of cotton. The cotton gin used a roller with metal teeth to scrape seeds off the cotton, and could do the work of dozens of slaves. Suddenly, American cotton exports grew from nearly zero in 1790 to 6 million pounds by 1796.

WORDS TO KNOW

with a vengeance: to an excessive or surprising degree.

skimp: to give someone a very small amount of something.

Farmers planted thousands of acres of cotton. The Deep South became a cotton kingdom. Human labor was needed to till and harvest the cotton and the decline of slavery quickly reversed. Soon, slavery spread to new territories south of the Ohio River. In 1790, 650,000 enslaved people lived in the South. By 1800, that number jumped 900,000. By 1820, there were 1.8 million slaves and by 1850, there were 3.2 million slaves. Slavery peaked at 4 million in 1860.

Rather than dying a slow death, the institution of slavery had been reborn with a vengeance.

LIFE AS A SLAVE

Not only did slaves have to work for free, they also had to behave a certain way. A slave had to lower his eyes in the presence of a white person and step off the path as a white person passed. Slaves were expected to be cheerful at all times. Owners thought that crabbiness and sadness might be signs that the slave was thinking about escape.

Slave vs. Free

Take a look at this timeline of how the nation became geographically divided by slavery. Look at the years each state was admitted into the country and whether it was a free or slave state. What does this timeline suggest about how politicians were trying to balance the demands of people who supported slavery with those who opposed slavery?

Learner coming of civil war 🔍

Often, owners disciplined slaves for no good reason. A woman named Fannie Moore was a slave on a Virginia plantation. She recalled the cruelty of the mother of her owner. The woman thought slaves were ". . . just like animals, not like other folks. She whip me, many time with a cow hide, till I was black and blue."

Gordon was a slave who escaped from Louisiana in 1863 and joined the Union Army. Photographs of his scarred back were used as a tool to convince people how bad slavery was.

Owners wanted to get the most amount of work out of their slaves for the least amount of cost. They **skimped** on slaves' food, clothing, and shelter. Fannie's master lived in a large, beautiful house while Fannie lived in a one-room cabin with a dirt floor. A slave cooked delicious multi-course meals for Fannie's owner. When it was time for Fannie's supper, her grandmother poured milk over a pot of cornbread, put several wooden spoons into the pot, and set it in the middle of the floor. The enslaved children dove at the pot, all eating at once.

Adult slaves were given one thin blanket and one or two sets of clothing each year. However, children too young to work in the fields were not given any blankets and received only one linen shirt. When this wore out, the child went naked.

Former slave Frederick Douglass (1818–1895) recalled how, "in hottest summer and coldest winter, I was kept almost naked—no shoes, no stockings, no jacket, no trousers, nothing on but a coarse tow linen shirt, reaching only to my knees." To stay warm at night, Douglass crawled inside a discarded sack.

Enslaved children as young as two were assigned physical tasks, such as hauling water and wood, picking up trash, and chasing birds out of the garden. Most children began field work between the ages of eight and twelve.

Although they were not physically behind bars, slaves were in a jail of sorts. They could not travel off their owner's property without a pass. Slaves were forbidden from gathering in groups. They could not buy or sell goods, carry a weapon, or ride a horse without their owner's **consent**. Enslaved couples could not legally marry. Slave children were not allowed to attend school or learn to read and write. Worst of all, an owner could sell off any family member at any time for any reason.

The brutality of daily life was unendurable for many enslaved people. Resistance was dangerous, but slaves fought back anyway. In the next chapter, you will examine how slaves **rebelled** against their captivity in many ways. Their **defiance** sparked some whites to come to the slaves' defense and other whites to hurt them even more.

Cultural Infusion

The cultural traditions that enslaved people inherited from their African ancestors **infused** American culture in many ways. Here are a few things in modern society that come from slave culture:

> Folktales—Brer Rabbit and Chicken Little

> Foods—black-eyed peas, kidney beans, yams, peanuts, and watermelon

> Expressions—bozo, funk, and zombie

> Musical styles—spirituals, jazz, and blues

> Instruments—banjo, fiddle, bells, and hand-clapping music or hambone

> Dance moves—jig, shuffle, and backstep

? ESSENTIAL QUESTION

Now it's time to consider and discuss the Essential Question: How did the U.S. Constitution enable Southern states to maintain the institution of slavery?

GRAPHING THE TRANSATLANTIC SLAVE TRADE

Historians used different types of data to make sense of the past. Stories of individual slave experiences provide a close-up view of life as an enslaved person, but a wide lens is also needed to understand the extent of global slavery. Statistical graphs can help historians interpret large numbers.

Look at this bar graph and use it to answer the questions below.

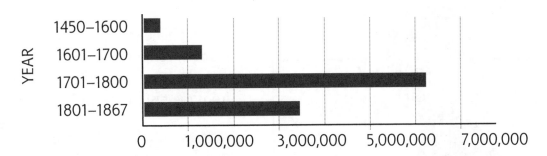

**The Atlantic Migration
Number of African Departures to
Western Hemisphere, 1450–1867**

NUMBER OF ENSLAVED AFRICANS IDENTIFIED
Total known population: 11,313,000

* What does this data tell you about slavery and how it changed during centuries?

* What factors might have caused more Africans to be transported during one century over another?

* What questions about slavery does this graph help answer and what questions does it not address?

* What math problems can you write and solve from the data on this chart?

EXPLORE MORE: One problem with statistics is that they are impersonal. How can you take this data about millions of Africans and put a human face on these victims of slavery?

ACTIVITY

COOK A HOE CAKE

The simple cornmeal pancake has long roots in America. It was George Washington's favorite breakfast. The dish gets its name from a flat pan called a hoe griddle. Enslaved people did not have this type of griddle. Instead, they baked their corn cakes on garden hoes in fires near the fields where they worked. Try your hand at cooking this staple of a slave's diet.

Find a recipe for hoe cake in *American Cookery* by Amelia Simmons, published in 1798, at this website.

Amelia Simmons hoe cakes 🔍

Do an online search for modern recipes for hoe cake. How do they differ from the historic recipe?

Choose one recipe to prepare and taste test.

* What does it taste like? Is it filling?

* Why might this food appeal to slaves who have to work all day?

EXPLORE MORE: Some recipes for hoe cake call for yeast. What function does yeast serve in bread recipes? Would enslaved people have used yeast? Why or why not?

Chapter 2

JOSIAH
HENSON
Price for
Freedom
~~$450~~
$1,000

RESISTANCE

Josiah Henson was Isaac Riley's prized possession. Strong, athletic, and **ambitious**, he could "out-hoe, out-reap, out-husk, out-dance . . ." every other slave. Riley made Henson overseer of his farm. Henson supervised the growing of crops, transported goods to market, and negotiated sales on Riley's behalf.

Eventually, Henson married an enslaved woman named Charlotte and they had four children. Skilled workers were valuable, and Henson was convinced no harm would ever come to his family.

But through the years, Riley fell into debt and needed to hide his slaves from his **creditors**. Riley ordered Henson to transport 18 slaves, including Henson's own wife and children, to the farm of Riley's brother in Kentucky.

? ESSENTIAL QUESTION

What are some of the ways different groups of people objected to slavery before the Underground Railroad began?

WORDS TO KNOW

ambitious: having a strong desire to become successful.

creditor: someone who is owed money.

rations: the food allowance for one day.

eavesdrop: to listen in on someone else's conversation.

literacy: the ability to read and write.

WORDS TO KNOW

During the journey, Henson had a chance to escape, but he did not take it.

He wanted freedom, but he believed the only honorable way to get it was to purchase himself. Henson got permission from Riley's brother to return to Maryland to negotiate for his freedom.

Riley agreed to let Henson buy himself for $450. Henson was short $100, but Riley said Henson could pay the rest of the money when he got it. He put Henson's freedom certificate in a sealed letter addressed to his brother and told Henson he would get the certificate upon return to Kentucky.

When Riley's brother opened the letter, Henson discovered he had been betrayed. There was no freedom certificate in the envelope. Instead, Riley had written his brother a note saying the price of Henson's freedom was $1,000. Henson would remain a slave until he could raise another $650. That would take a lifetime.

Knowing Henson would be enraged at the treachery, Riley had instructed his brother to sell Henson. At that moment, Henson abandoned any idea of honor. As soon as he had the chance, he decided, he would run.

DID YOU KNOW?

This website features an exhibit of objects from African American history. Explore the collections of items that relate to the arts, communities, segregation, and slavery. How do the items relate to each other across their points in history? How do the echoes of slavery travel into this century?

National Museum African American History 🔍

DAY-TO-DAY DEFIANCE

Even before slaves began escaping on the Underground Railroad, people were standing up against the practice of slavery in many different ways. From the moment slavery began in America, enslaved people found ways to resist their bondage.

Some resistance was hard for owners to detect. For example, one day, Jacob Stroyer decided he had been whipped too many times by a cruel overseer. When the man was not looking, Stroyer tied the overseer's whip to a piece of iron and threw it in the river. Of course, the overseer could just buy another whip, but for a few days, he could not lash his slaves.

Sometimes, if an owner increased the workload too much, slaves slowed their pace, broke tools, or faked illness. If food **rations** were too skimpy, slaves snuck vegetables from the garden or food from the pantry. The law said no one could teach a slave to read or write, but when the house slave dusted the schoolroom, she might **eavesdrop** on a white child's lesson. The slave who worked the docks might steal a book and teach himself to read.

Enslaved people knew literacy was a powerful weapon in their fight for freedom.

Many masters required slaves to attend church services led by pro-slavery preachers. But slaves secretly gathered deep in the woods or met at night to hold their own prayer meetings. They snuck off the plantation to hear traveling ministers preach messages about how God was the real master of everyone, free and slave, black and white. Religious faith gave enslaved people hope. Sometimes, these preachers led slaves to do more than pray.

WORDS TO KNOW

rebellion: violent resistance to authority.

fanatic: a person who is wildly enthusiastic or obsessed about only one thing.

REVOLT

On a steamy summer night in 1831, a Virginia slave named Nat Turner (1800–1831) launched a bloody **rebellion** that struck terror into the hearts of slave owners everywhere.

Turner had been deeply religious since childhood. In 1825, he began having visions, which made him believe that God was telling him what to do. Turner began to preach and gained a large following. On August 22, he gave the call to strike.

At 2 a.m., Turner and four other slaves crept into the home of Joseph Travis, Turner's owner, and killed the entire family, including a baby in a cradle. Then they moved on to other houses. By noon, the army of slaves had grown to 60 armed men. They attacked 15 houses and killed 60 white people before they were stopped.

The backlash from Turner's Rebellion was swift. Turner was caught and hanged and his corpse was skinned. Across the South, mobs of angry whites attacked any blacks they found. In the town of Murfreesboro, Tennessee, a black man was beheaded for predicting that someday there would be a war between whites and blacks. In Richmond, North Carolina, all free blacks in the city were arrested. More than 200 innocent blacks were killed by whites in the aftermath of Turner's Rebellion.

Whites insisted that Turner had been crazy. Only insanity could explain his desire to be free. Slaveholders frequently tried to paint slavery as the natural condition of black people, insisting that slaves would be perfectly content if **fanatics** such as Turner would stop stirring them up.

After Turner's Rebellion, the movement of slaves throughout the South was restricted. Owners could no longer voluntarily free their slaves unless the state government approved it. Newly freed slaves had to leave the state at once or face re-enslavement. Any white person who supported efforts to abolish slavery was labeled the enemy.

Turner's Rebellion was not the first attempted slave revolt, nor was it the last. Violent uprisings by slaves were not common, however, and they all failed. The uprisings do reveal how determined enslaved people were to be free.

DID YOU KNOW?

Look at this timeline of the most significant slave rebellions in American history. Do these rebellions have anything in common? Which one came closest to success?

timeline of slave rebellions 🔍

Cure For What Ails You

Dr. Samuel Cartwright (1793–1863) of New Orleans developed a theory that the only reason a slave would want to escape was if they were mentally ill. Cartwright called the illness "drapetomania." The cure for the first attempt to run was food and shelter. The cure for the second attempt was "vigorous whippings." Why was this a useful diagnosis for slave owners?

equivocate: to conceal your true opinion.

minority: less than half of the population of a country.

revival: when something becomes popular after a long time of not being popular.

WORDS TO KNOW

ABOLITIONISTS

On January 1, 1831, the people of Boston woke up to discover there was a new newspaper in town—*The Liberator*. In the first issue, the publisher, William Lloyd Garrison (1805–1879), made it clear that a powerful new voice was on the scene. He warned his readers that his opposition to slavery would be brutally honest. "I am in earnest—I will not **equivocate**—I will not excuse—I will not retreat a single inch—AND I WILL BE HEARD." From 1831 through the end of the Civil War in 1865, Garrison published *The Liberator* every single week for a total of 1,820 issues. He was part of the abolitionist movement.

Determined to destroy slavery, this movement transformed the debate about slavery from a war of words into one of action.

The Liberator (December 15, 1854)

A small **minority** of people who opposed slavery had always existed in the United States. The strongest and earliest resistance to slavery came from a small Christian sect called the Quakers.

Colonizing Liberia

The American Colonization Society was formed in 1816. Members believed slavery should end, but they were afraid that if it ended suddenly, there might be a race war. They thought that if owners gradually and voluntarily freed their slaves and relocated them on another continent, slavery would end peacefully. The organization established a colony on the west coast of Africa. By 1867, more than 13,000 African Americans had relocated to this nation, called Liberia. However, most blacks had no desire to move. They were Americans and wanted to remain free and equal in the United States.

Quaker communities practiced total nonviolence. They considered dancing and music silly and vain. Most importantly, Quakers believed the light of God shone in every person's soul. No one could own God, therefore, no one should own another human being. By the end of the eighteenth century, Quaker communities across the country had freed their slaves.

In 1775, Quakers formed the nation's first abolitionist organization—the Pennsylvania Society for Promoting the Abolition of Slavery. By 1800, there were anti-slavery societies in almost every state. As a religious **revival** spread throughout America in the 1820s, other Christian groups joined antislavery efforts.

Pressure from opponents of slavery led Northern states to abolish slavery or pass gradual emancipation laws. These laws declared that, after a certain date, children born to enslaved mothers were free. But the process of abolishing slavery was slow and varied from state to state. As late as 1860, 18 slaves still lived in New Jersey.

radical: someone who wants major change in social, political, or economic systems.

morally: from the point of view of right and wrong action or good and bad character.

sinfulness: evil.

WORDS TO KNOW

Frustrated by the slow pace of change, a small group of **radical** abolitionists emerged in the 1830s. These radicals wanted slavery destroyed quickly and completely. However, abolitionists were a small group and lived scattered about the country. They had no power.

That was soon to change. William Lloyd Garrison, publisher of *The Liberator*, organized the New England Antislavery Society in 1832. Lewis Tappan (1788–1873) and Arthur Tappan (1786–1865), a pair of wealthy brothers, started a similar group in New York. Garrison believed abolitionists would have greater power if they were united. He organized a national convention to be held in Philadelphia in December 1833.

The city was tense as the delegates arrived. Most Americans thought abolitionists were crazy. Newspapers described them as dangerous fanatics.

The police warned the convention leaders that they would not guarantee the delegates' safety, but the delegates still came.

The people who attended the convention all came from Northern states. Most were young, male, and white, and many were Quakers. There were a handful of free blacks in the group and a few women. The delegates met for three days straight, not even breaking for meals. When hungry, they nibbled on crackers and drank water.

The delegates formed a new national organization—the American Antislavery Society. The mission statement of this society formed the principles that inspired workers on the Underground Railroad. It challenged people to take direct action to end slavery, but rejected violence. Instead, the society believed slavery could be overcome by making owners see that slavery was **morally** wrong. The convention adjourned with the pledge to found anti-slavery societies in "every city, town, and village."

Hundreds of anti-slavery societies were created across Northern communities. Dozens of anti-slavery newspapers were established. Thousands of pamphlets were passed out. In 1835, abolitionists flooded the mailboxes of slaveholders with warnings to repent their evil ways. Abolitionists launched the Great Petition Campaign in 1836 and sent a wave of citizen requests to Congress demanding an end to slavery. In 1838, Congress received so many petitions they filled a 20-by-30-foot room from floor to ceiling.

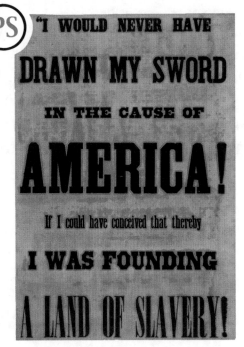

A poster from the anti-slavery movement

Traveling agents did the grunt work of the abolitionist movement. Many of these men were preachers. They traveled for months on end, speaking about the **sinfulness** of slavery. Their work helped convince people in rural areas of the North to oppose slavery. The agents raised money and got petitions signed. By 1837, there were more than 100,000 members of the American Antislavery Society and more than 1,000 local abolitionist organizations spread across the Northern states.

hostility: great anger or strong dislike.

tarred and feathered: a form of mob punishment where pine tar, a thick, sticky substance, is heated and poured over a person, after which the individual is covered in feathers.

ransack: to search for something in a way that messes up or damages the place being searched.

gag rule: a law that prevents people from talking about a specific subject.

convert: to change.

urgency: needing immediate attention.

WORDS TO KNOW

Hostility greeted abolitionists wherever they went. In slave states, mobs attacked post offices and burned all abolitionist pamphlets. White Southerners suspected of abolitionist views were harassed, arrested, and even **tarred and feathered**.

Northern audiences were no more welcoming. In Hartford, Connecticut, the First Congregational Church, where anti-slavery meetings were held, was burned. In Cincinnati, Ohio, law enforcement stood by as white mobs burned black neighborhoods. Elijah Lovejoy, a white editor of an anti-slavery publication in Alton, Illinois, was shot to death as he tried to defend his office from being **ransacked** by an angry mob.

The national government was no help. In 1836, Congress passed a **gag rule** prohibiting the discussion of all abolitionist petitions before the House of Representatives. By the end of the 1830s, abolitionists realized that the American public, the law, and the government were on the side of slavery. Something had to change.

AFRICAN AMERICAN LEADERS STIR THINGS UP

Black abolitionists who had escaped slavery grew impatient with the slow pace of freedom. Frederick Douglass, Henry Highland Garnett (1815–1882), and Sojourner Truth (1797–1883) used their personal stories to persuade people to support a more aggressive approach to freeing slaves.

Feminist Abolitionist

Even though politics was considered a man's game in nineteenth-century America, Lucretia Mott (1793–1880) and a handful of other women attended the anti-slavery convention in Philadelphia in 1833. Mott even addressed the audience. Following the convention, Mott founded the Philadelphia Female Anti-Slavery Society. This all-female, interracial organization existed until 1870.

Frederick Douglass could move an audience from outrage to tears. The first time he stepped in front of a podium, Douglass trembled with nerves, but he wanted to tell his story. He was born on a Maryland plantation in 1818 and escaped in 1838. He told his audiences about being so hungry when he was a child that he fought the dog for table scraps. People wept as Douglass described the time he witnessed his aunt stripped to the waist, tied to a beam, and whipped until her back was shredded.

Other former slaves took their stories on the road. Some listeners were **converted** to abolitionism, while others threw rotten eggs or stones. The testimony of these former slaves brought energy and **urgency** to the abolitionist movement. By the 1840s, white leaders were ready to start acting to help slaves. Their timing was perfect. A system was already developing to do just that—the Underground Railroad.

? ESSENTIAL QUESTION

Now it's time to consider and discuss the Essential Question: What are some of the ways different groups of people objected to slavery before the Underground Railroad began?

WHO GOES THERE?

Owners could hire out their slaves to work for someone else. Some hired-out slaves were required to be licensed and to wear an identification tag at all times. The medallions were small copper squares, between 1½ and 3 inches square, worn around the neck on a string or chain. The badges were engraved with a few simple words, including the city where the slave lived, an identification number, job title, and the year.

Slave badge (Collection of the Smithsonian National Museum of African American History and Culture)

Look at this slave badge. Historians are left with a mystery. Who was the person who wore this badge? Did he have a family? Did he ever get his freedom? What were his hopes and dreams? What were his nightmares? If you had to wear an ID tag that would communicate who you are to the future, what would that tag say?

Make your own identity tag using a similar method as the slave badges, but reveal more about who you are as a person. What key words reveal who you are? Here are two examples of personal badges.

Jon Hanson

* Older brother
* Shortstop
* Dreamer

Esme Garcia

* Mexican American
* Cat lover
* Skateboarder

DID YOU KNOW?

The importation of slaves into the United States was banned after 1808. Take a look at the animated map on this website. What do you see happening after 1808? Was the law against importing slaves enforced?

slave voyages database animated map 🔍

EXPLORE MORE: How do people react when they read your ID? Do they see you the way you see yourself? Ask your friends what four descriptors they would use to describe you. Do you agree with their descriptions of you?

BROADCAST YOUR VIEWS ON A BROADSIDE

Broadsides were posters that could have both words and pictures. They were the main source of information in the days before radio, television, and the Internet. During the time of slavery, broadsides were displayed in courthouses or post office buildings, hung in shop windows, and handed out on the street. In this activity, you will make your own broadside.

Take a look at this broadside.

* What can you tell about who produced this broadside?

* What does this broadside want people to do?

* How do the authors of this broadside feel about slavery and abolitionists?

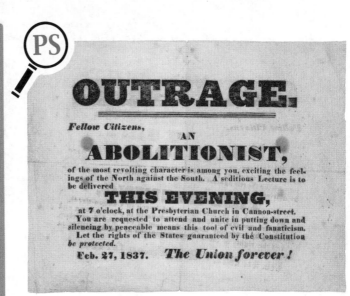

(Rare Book and Special Collections Division, Library of Congress)

If you could abolish anything in the world, what would it be? Draw your own broadside to persuade people to agree with you on this issue.

EXPLORE MORE: Historic broadsides were displayed on paper. You live in an electronic age and have more choices available to you. Create a digital broadside. What form will it take? How will you distribute it? Are there advantages and disadvantages to digital publishing? What are the advantages and disadvantages of paper broadsides?

WORDS TO KNOW

broadside: an advertisement or public notice printed on a large piece of paper and displayed for public viewing.

Chapter 3

LAYING THE TRACKS

Josiah Henson stole away with his family on a dark, moonless, September night in 1830. The Riley farm was near the Ohio River, and Henson begged another slave to row the family across. As they climbed aboard the **skiff**, the man whispered, "You'll not be brought back alive, will you?"
"Not if I can help it," Henson replied.

The family sat as still as death, the only sound the whisper of the oars in the water. When Henson's feet touched the shore of Indiana, he ". . . began to feel that I was my own master." But it was too early to celebrate. Although Indiana was a free state, it was full of slavery supporters. If the wrong person spotted them, the Henson family was doomed. Hiding by day, walking by night, they headed east toward Cincinnati, Ohio, 150 miles away.

THE FIRST TRAIN LEAVES THE STATION

Since the Underground Railroad was not a real train, no whistle blew and no conductor called, "All aboard." Historians have had to hunt for evidence about where this undercover operation began. All clues point to Philadelphia, Pennsylvania.

At the turn of the nineteenth century, the city was the place to be for young men in search of fortune. Philadelphia was the nation's first capital. Members of Congress strolled down the streets alongside European **immigrants**, Quakers in broad-brimmed hats, and free African Americans.

Slavery still existed in Pennsylvania, but it was dying out. In 1780, the state passed the first state Abolition Act. Vermont had already abolished slavery through its state constitution, in 1777. In Pennsylvania, slaves born before 1780 had to remain slaves, but those born after that date would become free on their 28th birthday. Most slave owners in Philadelphia had voluntarily freed their slaves by 1800.

Isaac Hopper (1771–1852), who was white, was only 17 years old in 1787 when he left his parents' home in New Jersey and moved to Philadelphia. When Hopper was seven years old, an elderly servant had brought the boy to tears when he told Hopper how he had been kidnapped from his home in Africa. From then on, Hopper felt a deep sympathy for the plight of slaves.

Isaac Hopper took his Quaker faith seriously and devoted his life to helping African Americans.

ESSENTIAL QUESTION

Why did the Underground Railroad start when it did? Why not sooner?

WORDS TO KNOW

unscrupulous: dishonest.

loophole: an error in a law that makes it possible for some people to legally disobey it.

collaborators: people who work together in order to achieve a goal.

document: to record.

In 1796, Hopper was elected to the Pennsylvania Abolition Society. **Unscrupulous** slave traders sometimes kidnapped free blacks and sold them into slavery. The Abolition Society gave him the job of investigating kidnapping cases and representing the African Americans in court. Hopper found every **loophole** within the law to help these people remain free. However, it did not take long for him to move from *using* the law to aid free blacks to *breaking* the law to help slaves escape to freedom.

Stories about Isaac Hopper and his small group of secret **collaborators** are the earliest **documented** records of the Underground Railroad. The people who worked with Hopper were from all races and economic levels. White Quaker farmers, black dock workers, and middle class shopkeepers joined forces. No single person was in charge. What united this handful of people was a moral belief that slavery was wrong.

DID YOU KNOW?

In 1796, no one used the term *Underground Railroad*. Trains had not even been invented!

Hopper and his colleagues worked out procedures that eventually became standard on all Underground Railroad routes. Fugitives were sent on foot, horseback, or wagon to a safe location. Disguises were used to confuse slave catchers.

Hopper even put a fugitive's freedom before his own safety. His home near the river in Philadelphia often sheltered runaways. Once, he sneaked up the stairs of a house and grabbed a pistol from a man who was whipping a slave girl. By the time Hopper died in 1852, he had saved hundreds, possibly even thousands, of runaway slaves and established a model of resistance.

In the early nineteenth century, Quakers made up only about 2 percent of the U.S. population, less than 100,000 people. However, Quakers kept strong ties with each other. They conducted monthly and yearly meetings when families gathered from all around the country. The work of the Philadelphia activists spread to other Quaker groups, and more track was laid for the Underground Railroad.

COMMUNITY OF QUAKERS

When Levi Coffin (1798–1877) was a young man, a wagon train of westward-bound settlers passed his home in New Garden, North Carolina. A short time later, a black man appeared on the road. He asked Levi how far ahead the wagons were. Levi told him and the man trudged on.

Dismal Swamp

Some slaves escaped to remote areas that were known as maroon communities. The largest of these was located in the Great Dismal Swamp, which covers part of Virginia and North Carolina. The swamp originally covered about 1.3 million acres, most of which was below water. The dry parts were home to wild cattle, bear, wolf, deer, and fugitive slaves. Whites believed the swamp gases poisoned the air, so they usually didn't go looking for runaways there. Today, 112,000 acres of the Dismal Swamp are preserved and archaeologists have found remains of settlements where generations of fugitives lived.

Later that day, Levi saw the man at the local blacksmith's shop with a white man. It turned out the man was a runaway. His wife and children had been sold to a family traveling west. The slave had chased after them, but he was caught. As Levi watched, the blacksmith attached a chain around the fugitive's neck and cuffed his wrists.

"Now you shall know what slavery is," the owner said. He tied one end of the chain to his buggy and whipped his horses into a trot. The slave had to run to keep up with the wagon or be dragged by his neck. This incident changed Levi Coffin's life.

When he was adult, Coffin was known for being someone fugitive slaves could turn to for help. In 1819, he and other Quakers came to the aid of a fugitive named John Dimery, the first runaway who used the Underground Railroad in North Carolina that historians can identify by name.

Dimery had been freed from slavery by his owner in another part of North Carolina. He moved to New Garden with his wife. When Dimery's prior owner died in 1819, his sons came looking for their father's former slave, hoping to sell him. They burst through Dimery's door in the middle of the night and seized him. Dimery yelled for his daughter to "fetch Mister Coffin."

Two Quakers caught up with the kidnappers at a neighbor's house. They demanded the men either release Dimery or appear before a judge to prove their claim that he was a slave.

Branching Out

It was not easy being an abolitionist in a state full of pro-slavery citizens. In 1826, Levi Coffin and his wife, Catherine, moved west to Fountain City, Indiana. The couple not only packed up their clothes, furniture, and farm tools, they also brought their wish to help runaways. Before long, the Coffin home was a key safe house for three routes for fugitives.

While the kidnappers debated what to do, a woman in the house untied Dimery's hands when no one was looking. He raced out the door, disappearing into the woods. Afraid they might be arrested, the kidnappers ran off. Decades later, Levi Coffin's uncle recalled that Dimery "started on the Underground Railroad that night and soon landed at Richmond, Indiana."

BLACK BUSINESSMEN TAKE THE LEAD

One of the most effective stops on the Underground Railroad is also one of the most mysterious—Madison, Indiana, 80 miles downriver from Cincinnati, Ohio. This stop was operated by a group of African Americans led by a freeborn black man named George DeBaptiste. None of the people involved in this network left written records about their activities, so historians are left with only fragments of evidence.

Madison had a population of 10,000 people in the early nineteenth century, and only 200 of them were African American. The town sat on the banks of the Ohio River. A small group of black businessmen worked together to help fugitives. George DeBaptiste ran a barbershop in the heart of town where he could listen for local gossip. John Carter, the owner of a market stall, received messages about runaways who needed help getting across the river.

WORDS TO KNOW

Stepney Stafford operated a laundry that was used by pro-slavery families. As the staff delivered the wash to these homes, they eavesdropped for word of slave catchers on the prowl. Elijah Anderson ran the blacksmith shop by day and conducted fugitives by night.

Two white men, John Todd and his brother, were also part of this circle of collaborators. When it was safe for a fugitive to cross the river, John beat on a brass pot and waved a lantern to his brother, who watched from the other side.

To help fugitive slaves was to put yourself in danger, especially if you were a free black.

In 1846, Kentucky slave owners and the pro-slavery citizens of Madison launched an effort to destroy the Underground Railroad in town. White mobs invaded the homes of free blacks. A conductor named Griffin Booth was almost drowned in the Ohio River. Elijah Anderson moved to another town and George DeBaptiste fled to Detroit, Michigan. However, other people filled their places and runaways could still find help from the black community in Madison.

Horse for Sale

When a fugitive was ready to run, an operator would send a message to George DeBaptiste in code that might read like this: *"Mahogany Stallion. Large. Just the thing for a minister. Can see him on Tuesday afternoon. Price $100."*

This told DeBaptiste that the fugitive was an adult male of mixed race, that a church member would be at a certain place on Tuesday afternoon with the fugitive, and that the slave had $100 of his own money.

STAIRS TO FREEDOM

In the small town of Ripley, Ohio, a red brick farmhouse sits atop a steep **bluff** that overlooks the town. More than 200 steps climb from the Ohio River to the front door of the house. This house belonged to Minister John Rankin in the early nineteenth century, and it was the heart of the early Underground Railroad in Ohio. John Rankin, his wife, Jean, and their 13 children helped as many as 2,000 fugitives during the course of 30 years.

At the time, Ripley had a population of 3,000 people. The local economy was based on boat building and hog butchering.

Certain conditions made Ripley a ripe location for Underground Railroad activity.

First, there were several anti-slavery ministers in town. Also, the town was home to between 150 and 200 politically active white abolitionists. Additionally, this region of Ohio had a small population of free blacks who lived along the river and were in the perfect position to aid runaways.

The Rankin family was always on duty. The nine sons shared a bedroom, with the three oldest sleeping in one double bed. They rotated positions every night. The son on the outside of the bed had to answer the door and transport any fugitives to the next safe house on the line. The daughters prepared the food, washed and mended fugitives' clothing, and provided medical care.

WORDS TO KNOW

immortalize: to be remembered forever.

heroine: a woman admired for bravery.

catalyst: an event that causes a change.

segregate: to separate people based on race, religion, ethnicity, or some other category.

slum: a crowded area of a city where poor people live and buildings are in bad condition.

One of the fugitives John Rankin assisted became **immortalized** in literature. On a bitterly cold night in the winter of 1838, a black woman carrying an infant walked toward the Kentucky side of the Ohio River. Suddenly, dogs began to bay. The woman raced to the water's edge, a plank in one hand, her baby in the other. With her first step on the ice, the woman's foot fell through. She yanked her leg up and ran toward the Ohio shore. Suddenly, she fell through the ice. Pushing her baby ahead of her on the ice, the fugitive levered herself up with the plank. She crept along on her belly until she finally reached the opposite shore and collapsed.

A slave catcher named Chancey Shaw watched. He had planned to grab the woman and return her for a reward. However, Shaw heard the baby whimper and something inside him thawed. He said, "Woman, you have won your freedom."

Then he pointed to the staircase leading to the Rankin house. "No [fugitive] has ever been got back from that house."

The fugitive eventually reached Canada. John Rankin told the story to abolitionist Harriet Beecher Stowe. She based the **heroine** of her 1852 anti-slavery novel on this fugitive, naming her Eliza.

The book, *Uncle Tom's Cabin*, became a bestseller around the world. It awakened Northern whites to the horrors of slavery, and angered Southern whites who thought the book was a pack of lies. This novel was one of the **catalysts** that started the Civil War.

URBAN UNDERGROUND

DID YOU KNOW?

The character of Uncle Tom in Harriet Beecher Stowe's novel was loosely based on the life of Josiah Henson.

In the 1830s, Manhattan was a very smelly place. The city had a population of 300,000, and no sewage system, no housing codes, and few police officers. The air smelled of human waste, unwashed bodies, pigs, and charcoal. Men hawked fresh oysters and young girls sold hot corn. On any given day, more than 900 cargo ships lined the waterfront of the East River.

Racism followed free blacks throughout the city. In order to vote, men had to own a certain amount of property. Because most blacks were poor, they could not vote. Schools were **segregated**, as were theaters, restaurants, and hotels. African Americans could only ride the horse-drawn buses if they clung to the outside of the carriage. Approximately 15,000 blacks crammed into a section of Manhattan that was dirty, poor, and crime-ridden. The "Gates of Hell" and "Brickbat Mansion" were the nicknames of **slum** apartment buildings.

An informal ring of thieves called the "New York Kidnapping club" prowled the city streets. This group of professional slave hunters, city police officers, and local lawyers kidnapped free blacks and sold them into slavery. A man could claim that a black person was his runaway slave simply by submitting a sworn statement to the court.

In the fall of 1835, some African Americans organized a group called the Friends of Human Rights. Their goal was to stop slave catchers from kidnapping free blacks. David Ruggles (1810–1849) led the group's Vigilance Committee. Ruggles had grown up in the North, never witnessing slavery. But he was determined to free as many slaves as he could.

Under Ruggles' leadership, the Vigilance Committee advertised descriptions of blacks who had been kidnapped, raised money to help fugitives, and hired lawyers to defend runaways.

Ruggles' home became Manhattan's main depot on the Underground Railroad. Fugitives from as far away as Philadelphia were directed to his house when they arrived in the city. He did not keep his activities a secret. One year, he rented an apartment only one block away from the busiest street in New York City.

A letter of introduction from David Ruggles helped fugitives once they left New York City. He had allies who could move fugitives farther up the East Coast and into Vermont and New Hampshire. Quaker towns and black settlements took in runaways bearing letters signed by David Ruggles. He did not live to see the end of slavery, though. Ruggles died in 1849, at the young age of 39.

The tracks of the Underground Railroad did not stay in place as real train tracks do. Because of the constant changes, runaways often had to find their own way for many miles. Navigational skills were vital if a fugitive was to survive. In the next chapter, you'll explore the routes runaways took and how they found their way on the journey to freedom.

ESSENTIAL QUESTION

Now it's time to consider and discuss the Essential Question: Why did the Underground Railroad start when it did? Why not sooner?

THUMBS UP OR THUMBS DOWN

Many Northerners loved *Uncle Tom's Cabin*. Southerners were known to hate it. A person's opinion of the book depended on whether the person was for or against slavery.

Read these two brief excerpts from reviews of the book. What words reveal which excerpt is from a Northern newspaper and which is from a Southern one?

Excerpt 1: "...It is, unquestionably, a work of genius . . . . It has the capital excellence of exciting the interest of the reader; this never stops or falters from the beginning to the end . . . . Another cause of the wide-spread popularity of Uncle Tom is its foundation in truth."

Excerpt 2: "We have said that Uncle Tom's Cabin is a fiction. It is a fiction throughout; a fiction in form; a fiction in its facts . . . and falsehood is its end . . . ."

EXPLORE MORE: Read a modern novel about slavery and write a review of the book. Some titles include *Copper Sun* by Sharon Draper, *Chains* by Laurie Halse Anderson, and *Day of Tears* by Julius Lester.

Ruggles and Douglass

In 1838, a young, escaped slave named Frederick Augustus Bailey knocked on David Ruggles' door. Bailey was determined to flee to Canada. A week spent with Ruggles changed American history. Ruggles helped Bailey find work in New Bedford, Massachusetts, and convinced him to shed his past as a slave. Bailey changed his name to Frederick Douglass and went on to become the most **influential** leader for African American rights in the nineteenth century.

WORDS TO KNOW

influential: having power to make changes.

CONSTRUCT A MINIATURE DISMAL SWAMP

The Great Dismal Swamp once covered more than 1 million acres, but during the centuries, the swamp has shrunk by tens of thousands of acres due to damming and draining. In 1974, the federal government established the Great Dismal Swamp National Wildlife Refuge to preserve the land and species that live there.

A swamp is an area of wet, spongy ground that grows woody plants, such as trees and shrubs. Much of the swamp is a wetland. Water covers the soil or is near the surface of the soil for much of the year. Wetlands support thousands of water and land animals and absorb and slow floodwaters.

Build your own Dismal Swamp model to see the water-soaking characteristics of a swamp. You'll need a container and materials for the land and the swamp.

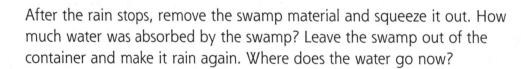

Construct your landform in half of your container and lay your swamp material alongside it in the rest of your container. Make it rain by sprinkling water over your miniature world. What happens to the water?

After the rain stops, remove the swamp material and squeeze it out. How much water was absorbed by the swamp? Leave the swamp out of the container and make it rain again. Where does the water go now?

EXPLORE MORE: Wetlands act as buffers to protect houses from flooding. Create a structure to represent a building and set that on your landform. What happens to that building when it rains hard when the swamp is in place? What about when the swamp is removed?

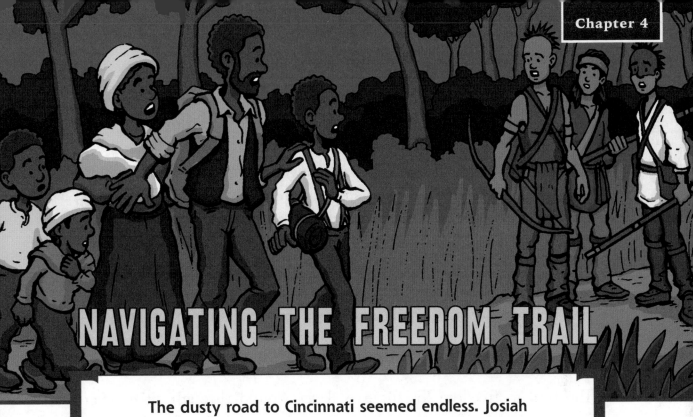

Chapter 4

NAVIGATING THE FREEDOM TRAIL

The dusty road to Cincinnati seemed endless. Josiah Henson led the way, carrying his youngest two children in a pack on his back. His wife followed with the two older children. Each day they walked more slowly, **fatigue** and hunger stealing their strength.

Finally, after 12 days on the road, the family ran out of food. They had to ask for help or starve to death. Josiah knocked on the door of a house. He had 25 cents to buy a bit of meat and bread.

This food carried the family to Cincinnati, where they were fed and sheltered by conductors on the Underground Railroad. After a short rest, helpers drove the Henson family 30 miles north and dropped them off. On their own again, the family resumed marching. That night, the family bedded down in the woods. Josiah hardly slept, startling awake at every rustle.

? ESSENTIAL QUESTION

What obstacles did fugitive slaves face in making their way to freedom and how did they overcome these obstacles?

fatigue: being very tired.

WORDS TO KNOW

The next morning, the family continued through the dense forest. Charlotte Henson fainted from exhaustion. Josiah's back was rubbed raw from where the pack dug into his skin. Just when they could not take another step, a group of Native Americans appeared on the trail. The two groups stared at each other for a long, tense moment. Then, recognizing that the family posed no threat, the Indians led the Hensons to a small village. They fed and sheltered the family, and the next day led the family to a lake and pointed north. Canada and freedom were still miles away.

WHICH WAY TO FREEDOM?

The trail to freedom for fugitive slaves wound through cities, over mountains, into forests, and across rivers and lakes. In the more heavily populated Eastern states, fugitives might travel by ship or train, but most often travel was the old fashioned way—in wagons, on horseback, and by foot.

The most heavily traveled lines of the Underground Railroad ran north, toward Canada. However, some fugitives escaped into the Western territories. Others sought freedom by sea and a few thousand Texan slaves fled south across the border into Mexico.

DID YOU KNOW?

Elijah Anderson, who lived north of Madison, Indiana, helped about 1,000 fugitives between 1839 and 1847. The Miller family from Medina County, Ohio, aided about 1,000 people during the course of 30 years working on the Underground Railroad.

The tracks of the Underground Railroad were always changing. As new lines opened, old ones closed. Sometimes, routes shut down because they became too dangerous. Other times, people who ran a line died or moved. Some paths were busy, while others saw very little activity.

THE NORTH

The most traveled road to freedom lay north. In the first decades of the nineteenth century, runaways found some freedom living in the Northern states, but, this freedom was fragile. The Fugitive Slave Law of 1793 allowed slave owners to pursue escaped slaves into free states and retrieve them. However, many free states passed personal liberty laws that made it easy for escaped slaves to keep from getting captured. Then, in 1850, a tougher fugitive slave law was passed, and no place in America was safe.

Canada, a British colony, became the best option for freedom. In 1791, John Graves Simcoe was appointed lieutenant governor of the colony. A fierce abolitionist, Simcoe vowed never to support a law that treated African Americans differently than whites. His declaration was followed by a series of court cases that gradually ended slavery in Canada. Then, in 1833, the British Empire abolished slavery in all its colonies, including Canada.

Word spread among American slaves that permanent freedom could be found in the neighbor to the North.

free soilers: people who opposed the spread of slavery into Western territories because they did not want small farmers to have to compete with richer farmers who could afford the free labor of slaves.

cutlass: a short sword with a curved blade.

arsenal: a place where weapons and military equipment are stored.

WORDS TO KNOW

The busiest gateway to Canada was through Detroit, Michigan. By 1837, there were 42 regularly scheduled steamboats that used the city's port. Black abolitionist William Lambert (1817–1890) led the city's Underground Railroad stop, aided by William Munroe, the minister of the Second Baptist Church. The church sheltered fugitives.

When night fell, a conductor led the runaways a few blocks to the waterfront. Across the Detroit River lay Canada, only a mile away. After a 10-minute ferry ride, runaway slaves became free.

THE WEST

In 1854, settlers organized the territory of Kansas. In order to gain statehood, territory leaders had to write a constitution. The people living in the territory had a huge debate about whether slavery should be legal in Kansas.

Missouri was next door to Kansas. In 1854, about 50,000 slaves lived there. Missourians did not want a free state so close, because it would make it too easy for Missouri slaves to escape. Northerners watched the debate with interest.

Many Northerners opposed any spread of slavery to the Western territories. Thousands of abolitionists and **free soilers** from the Northeast packed up their belongings and moved west. Their goal was to elect anti-slavery leaders who would write a constitution making Kansas a free state. Once they arrived in Kansas, some of these immigrants organized a western branch of the Underground Railroad.

A free soiler named James Lane (1814–1866) blazed a trail through Kansas. His goal was to lead immigrants from the East away from the pro-slavery settlements. Rock piles called "Lane's chimneys" marked the trail from Iowa into Kansas and Nebraska. After 1856, this trail was mostly abandoned by white immigrants, but during the next four years, runaway slaves might have used it to escape into the West.

Among the free soilers who moved to Kansas was a radical abolitionist named John Brown (1800–1859) and five of his sons. After the anti-slavery town of Lawrence was damaged by pro-slavers in December 1855, Brown led a raiding party to get revenge. On May 23, 1856, Brown and his men attacked a pro-slavery settlement, hacking five men to death with **cutlasses**.

> **Brown escaped a manhunt that pursued his gang, remaining free to carry out his next plan—to start a war to end slavery.**

On October 17, 1859, Brown and 16 followers, white and black men, launched a raid on Harpers Ferry, Virginia. Their goal was to seize the weapons stored in the federal **arsenal** there, arm local slaves, and begin a war to end slavery.

treason: the crime of betraying one's country.

sparse: few and scattered thinly over a wide area.

cede: to give up power over a territory to another country.

migrate: to move from one area to another.

WORDS TO KNOW

The raid was a failure. No local slaves rose up to join the rebellion. The U.S. Marines quickly surrounded the arsenal, and after a shootout, Brown was captured.

Convicted of **treason**, Brown went willingly to the hangman's noose, insisting to the end that, "If it is . . . necessary that I should forfeit my life for . . . justice, I say let it be done." Even though it was a failure, John Brown's raid put another wedge between the free North and slave South, and brought the United States one step closer to the Civil War.

THE SOUTH

Florida was the first promised land for American slaves. In colonial times, Florida was controlled by Spain and the Seminole Indians. Although slavery was legal in Spanish lands, in 1693, the Spanish government proclaimed that all American slaves who reached Florida and converted to the Catholic religion could live there as free people.

Adios, Master!

Canada is a long way from Texas, so Texan slaves ran south instead of north. Mexico abolished slavery in 1829 and refused to return any American slaves who sought refuge within its borders. There was no organized Underground Railroad along the southern border of the United States. This was a **sparsely** populated, wild frontier. Slaves had to rely on individual acts of kindness from people they encountered. Historians do not know for certain how many American slaves escaped into Mexico, but estimates suggest at least 4,000.

Fugitives from the Carolinas and Georgia took up the invitation. Spanish control of Florida did not last long, however. Spain **ceded** the territory to the United States, and thereafter, many blacks **migrated** from Florida to Cuba, another Spanish colony.

Even after the Spanish ceded Florida, fugitives found refuge among the 5,000 Seminole Indians who controlled the interior of the state. Although these Native Americans technically considered the runaways their slaves, life was better under the Seminoles than it had been with white owners. Fugitives lived in separate communities alongside the Seminoles, and they were allowed to develop their own community governments, carry weapons, and control their own labor as long as they paid a portion of their crops each year as tribute.

Some Seminole Indians and blacks married. Children of these couples became known as Black Seminoles.

DID YOU KNOW?

Another word for Black Seminoles is "Maroon," and possibly comes from the Spanish word, *cimarron*, meaning "untamed."

WORDS TO KNOW

haven: a place where a person is protected from danger.

hijack: to steal or kidnap.

technology: tools, methods, and systems used to solve a problem or do work.

Determined to gain solid control of all of Florida, the United States battled the Seminoles in a series of wars in the early 1800s. The Seminoles lost and were relocated to territory in the west. Florida was no longer a safe **haven**, but runaways still tried to sail to freedom along what was called the Saltwater Railroad.

WATER ROUTES

In 1859, William Peel had himself wrapped in straw, packaged in a crate, and shipped north by steamship. He was one of many fugitives who escaped via a waterway. Virginia records from the eighteenth century reveal that 14 percent of runaways were people with jobs either on the water or near it. Oyster fishermen stole skiffs and rowed to safety. Laundresses for crews delivered clean laundry to ships and then stowed away rather than disembarking.

DID YOU KNOW?

Explore the Underground Railroad with this interactive map. Which direction do most of the paths go? Why?

Eduplace Underground Railroad map

Ship pilots hijacked vessels and sailed them into Northern waters.

Free blacks were able to help runaways. The largest cities of the South were ports that shipped agricultural products to Europe and the Northern states. Blacks worked as ship caulkers, carpenters, fishermen, sailmakers, and dockworkers. Some vessels had all-black crews. These men hid fugitives onboard among bales of cotton and sacks of rice.

COMMUNICATION AND MAPPING

Imagine that you didn't travel and you didn't have access to books, television, the Internet, or any other communication. Would you know what states bordered yours and what mountains, deserts, or rivers were located near you?

Many enslaved people were completely isolated. They never went to school and were forbidden by law to learn to read. Many never set foot off the plantations where they were born. Slaves who wanted to escape did not have access to our modern **technology**, such as cell phones or GPS. They did not even have maps to guide them or anyone to ask for directions. Enslaved people and their allies on the Underground Railroad developed a series of verbal and written codes to help them navigate the journey to freedom.

Technology shapes the way we talk. In the last decade, new phrases have been added to our language, including "google it," "LOL," and "hashtag." These words come from social media. The technological breakthrough of the early nineteenth century was the railroad. The nation's first railroad began on a 1-mile track near Baltimore in 1830, with five train cars pulled by a horse. By 1840, 3,000 miles of track had been laid.

When to Run

Most slaves plotted their escape very carefully. Many ran during the Christmas season because they were often given passes to travel to nearby plantations to visit family members. An absence might not be noticed for several days. Late fall was another common time for escape because farmers had stored their harvest and runaways could survive on stolen crops.

metaphor: a figure of speech in which a word is used to symbolize another word.

imposter: a person pretending to be someone else.

documentation: a written record of something.

WORDS TO KNOW

Soon, a not-so-secret code sprang up, rooted in railroad **metaphors**. Safe houses were called "depots" or "stations," and the people who ran them were "stationmasters." Guides were called "conductors." Wagons used to transport fugitives were labeled "train cars" and the runaways were "passengers." People who donated money to help fugitives were "stockholders." Escape routes were called "tracks" or "lines."

Slave catchers sometimes hired free blacks to pose as runaways in order to trap railroad agents. To safeguard against this, agents on some lines gave fugitives a coin with a hole drilled in it. They handed this coin to the agent at their next stop, proving that they were not **imposters**.

Some agents marked the route when the terrain was hard to navigate. Abolitionists in rural North Carolina developed a system to guide the fugitives through the dense woods. When runaways arrived at a fork in the road, they were instructed to wrap their arms around the trees on each side of the fork and rub down slowly.

They would find a nail driven into the trunk of a tree on the correct path. If there were no trees at a fork, agents drove nails into fence posts—the second rail from the top—or used a large stone to identify the correct road. Why was this a better method than printing maps?

The natural world was another tool that fugitives used to point themselves north. In the summer, migrating birds flew north. In some areas, moss grew on the north side of dead trees.

The North Star was a beacon in the night sky, visible on all but the cloudiest of nights.

The North Star, also known as Polaris, is fixed—its position in the sky never changes. One way to find the North Star is to find the constellation known as the Big Dipper or Ursa Major. These stars outline the shape of a bowl with a handle. The two bright stars in the front of the bowl point to Polaris. Some slaves were able to find this star and follow its lead to the Northern states.

The North Star led Thomas Cole out of slavery in Alabama when he was only 16. Life had been tolerable for many years. Thomas's owner never whipped his slaves and he did not break apart families. But one summer, Thomas's owner died. Thomas was left to work on the plantation under a cruel overseer.

Myth Buster: Slave Quilts

In 1994, a journalist named Jacqueline Tobin bought a quilt from a woman who said that her family told of ancestors who used patterns in quilts to communicate messages to runaways. Tobin wrote a book about this family, and the media latched onto the idea. Soon, elementary school children were being taught about codes in slave quilts as a proven fact. That is not the case.

Historians require **documentation** from many sources to develop a convincing argument about the past. So far, no evidence about quilts has been found. Messages in slave quilts remain part of the myth of the Underground Railroad, not part of its history.

abruptly: all of a sudden.

patrol: people who systematically checked different areas in search of runaway slaves.

WORDS TO KNOW

By this time, the Civil War had begun, and times were hard. Food was in short supply. One day, the overseer sent Thomas and some other slaves to hunt for deer in nearby woods. Thomas seized his chance. "I crosses de river and goes north . . . I travels all dat day and night up de river and follows de north star."

Thomas ran into two Union soldiers. He joined the Union Army and fought at the Battle of Chickamauga in Tennessee. After the Union won the war, Thomas married, had two children, and moved to Texas, where he farmed a small plot of land.

DID YOU KNOW?

Go outside on a clear night and look up. How many stars can you see? Scientists have calculated the naked eye can see 9,096 stars. Can you find Polaris?

Like Thomas, many slaves decided to run **abruptly**. They might find out they were going to be sold or loved ones were going to be sold. They might be facing a whipping or they might suddenly decide to take their chances in the hope of freedom. Many slaves heard about opportunities for fleeing and realized they had to make a move.

It was always a dangerous decision, though. Danger lurked around every bend for escaping slaves. Night **patrols**, slave catchers, and bloodhounds pursued fugitives and their allies. The next chapter explores the hazards fugitives faced and how runaways and Underground Railroad operators developed strategies for outwitting their hunters.

? ESSENTIAL QUESTION

Now it's time to consider and discuss the Essential Question: What obstacles did fugitive slaves face in making their way to freedom and how did they overcome these obstacles?

WRITE A CODED MESSAGE

Harriet Tubman, a famous Underground Railroad conductor, sometimes used code phrases to communicate with her helpers. Use the following phrases that might have been Underground Railroad codes to write a secret message. Pretend that you are an agent writing to a stationmaster in another city.

* agent: someone who coordinates escapes for slaves.

* baggage, boxes, parcels, packages, passengers: fugitive slaves.

* brakeman: someone who helps fugitives find jobs and homes when they reach freedom.

* conductor: a person who guides or escorts slaves.

* Heaven, promised land, Canaan: Canada.

* forward: to move slaves between stations.

* freedom train: Underground Railroad.

* Moses: Harriet Tubman.

* station: a safe place where fugitives are hid and sheltered.

* stationmaster: someone who provides shelter for fugitives.

* stockholder: someone who donates money or goods to the cause.

* "The wind blows from the south today": runaway slaves are in the area.

* "A friend with friends": a password used by a conductor arriving with fugitives.

* "Lost a passenger": a runaway slave has been caught.

Give the message to another person who has read this book and see if they can decipher the message without looking up the definitions to the words.

EXPLORE MORE: In the Underground Railroad, codes were used by people who were resisting the government in order to help fugitive slaves. But government officials have also used codes throughout American history, most often during wars to confound the enemy. Research the role that codes have played in military conflicts, from the spy network of General George Washington in the Revolutionary War to the Navajo Code Talkers of World War II. What impact did secret communications have in these conflicts?

FIND POLARIS

Before a fugitive slave could follow Polaris to freedom, he first had to locate it in the night sky. Polaris has a fixed position. This means its location in the sky does not change with the seasons the way other constellations do. However, the sky is crowded with stars and it takes practice locating Polaris. The key to finding it is to use the constellation called the Big Dipper.

Use this chart to help you locate the North Star. The North Star stays in the same position while the Big and Little Dippers rotate around it as the seasons pass.

Go outside on a clear night. Locate the two constellations called the Big Dipper and Little Dipper.

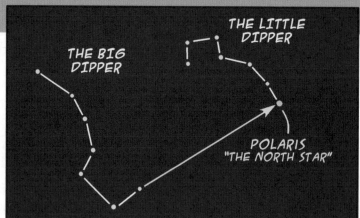

Follow the lower right corner of the Big Dipper and trace it with your eye to the top of the handle of the Little Dipper. That is Polaris.

Try walking toward Polaris. Is it easy to keep the star in sight as you walk? Does the star appear closer as you move?

Look elsewhere in the sky and walk in a different direction. Now try to locate Polaris again. How easy is it for you to find the star. Imagine you can hear the baying of hounds in the distance and you know slave catchers are hunting you. How might fear of recapture impact your ability to navigate by the night sky?

ACTIVITY

FOLLOW THE DRINKING GOURD

According to legend, Peg Leg Joe, a black man with one leg, worked as a traveling handyman. He moved from plantation to plantation teaching slaves a song called "Follow the Drinking Gourd." Stories about this song claim it was a coded message used to guide slaves north. However, there is very little evidence that this is true. It can be difficult to separate fact from myth when discussing the Underground Railroad, since so little of the history was written down. We might never know what role, if any, "Follow the Drinking Gourd" played in history. However, the exercise of decoding the song requires you to break apart the lyrics and apply what you know about the way the Underground Railroad worked, and it is fun!

Go to this link and listen to the song while reading the accompanying lyrics.

follow the drinking gourd 🔎

★ Why do you think the myth that this song was part of the Underground Railroad has persisted?

★ How would this message help slaves preparing to escape?

★ What geographical clues are woven into the lyrics?

EXPLORE MORE: Write your own coded song. Choose a popular tune and rewrite the lyrics to guide people to a well-known place. Sing this song for a friend and see if he or she can figure out what location you are guiding them to.

WORDS TO KNOW

gourd: a plant with a hard shell that is related to cucumbers and melons, but is not edible.

Chapter 5

TREACHEROUS TRAVEL

Fear perched on Josiah Henson's shoulder throughout his journey north. The trail through the Ohio wilderness was a never-ending maze. The cries of hunger from his children were blows to Josiah's heart, and the threat of capture haunted his every step. Josiah recalled, "A fearful dread of detection ever pursued me, and I would start out of my sleep in terror, my heart beating against my ribs, and expecting to find the dogs and slave-hunters after me."

Henson had reason to fear. As the nineteenth century progressed and the activities of the Underground Railroad increased, slave owners pressured the federal government to pass laws to protect their slave property. By 1850, both fugitives and anyone who helped them were at great risk.

? ESSENTIAL QUESTION

Why would slaves risk the dangers of escape to gain their freedom?

FUGITIVE SLAVE LAW

Escape to a free state did not make a slave free. The Constitution guaranteed slave owners the right to take back their escaped slaves. The 1793 Fugitive Slave Act authorized the arrest of runaways throughout the United States, while a free person who aided a fugitive could be fined $50. But under the 1793 law, hunting down a runaway was the slave owner's responsibility.

A slave was considered private property and the return of an escaped slave was considered a private act. The sheriff and police department were not required to launch a search. Slaveholders had to search on their own or hire a slave catcher. As the Underground Railroad expanded and more fugitives escaped, Southerners demanded something be done to stop this loss of property.

In 1848, the United States won a war with Mexico and gained vast stretches of land in the Southwest. The debate over whether these lands should be slave or free states threatened to split the nation apart. Political leaders tried to solve the problem by passing the Great Compromise in 1850. Part of this compromise included a new, harsher fugitive slave law.

A Drop in the Bucket

It's impossible to know exactly how many enslaved people escaped in the years before the Civil War began in 1861. Many records didn't survive history and escaped slaves needed to keep quiet, anyway. Estimates range between 1,000 and 5,000 a year from 1830 to 1860. That means between 30,000 and 150,000 slaves escaped, which is a drop in the bucket compared with the 4 million slaves who lived in the United States in 1860.

The 1850 Fugitive Slave Law stacked the dice against black people, both free and enslaved. The private responsibility of a slave owner to find his runaway slave was transformed into the government's job. An owner could get a **warrant** and demand assistance from federal court commissioners to find and arrest suspected fugitives. The commissioners relied on a general description of the escaped slave, such as gender, skin tone, age, and scars to identify the slaves they were searching for.

When a free African American matched the vague description of a fugitive, he was often arrested. Do you think this was fair?

The Fugitive Slave Law had a built-in **incentive** for **commissioners** to ignore cases of mistaken identity. They were paid $10 for every fugitive returned to an owner, but only $5 for ruling that the arrested person was not the runaway. Free blacks faced the real threat of being enslaved. When someone was arrested on suspicion of being a fugitive, he or she did not get a jury trial. Instead, the case was heard before a judge whose **verdict** could not be **appealed**. The Fugitive Slave Law sent free blacks fleeing to Canada in droves.

DID YOU KNOW?

Instead of derailing the Underground Railroad, more tracks were laid, more agents became active, and more enslaved people escaped from slavery.

**Life had suddenly become
far too dangerous in the United States
for anyone with dark skin.**

SLAVE WATCHERS AND SLAVE HUNTERS

John Capeheart was a police officer in Norfolk, Virginia, in the 1850s. He also worked as a **freelance** slave hunter. One of Capeheart's tasks was to arrest all blacks who gathered in groups at night. These people did not need to be doing anything wrong. To be black and gathered in a group of more than two or three people was a crime in many states at this time.

Capeheart did not need warrants. He earned 50 cents for every black person he arrested. They would spend the night in jail, and the next morning Capeheart would take them to the mayor who assigned punishment. Capeheart carried out the sentence—**flogging**. He was paid an additional 50 cents for every person he whipped.

John Capeheart was part of the system Southern states used to terrorize blacks, prevent escapes, and make the capture of runaways easier. In port cities, black travelers and workers were immediately arrested if they did not carry papers proving they were free or had permission to travel. Steamboats were searched for stowaways.

patroller: a person who walks around an area to make sure rules are being obeyed.

WORDS TO KNOW

Communities also had **patrollers**, sometimes called paddy rollers. These squads had legal authority to monitor the movements of black people, slave or free. Patrollers could come to anyone's property and search any buildings without a warrant. They could shoot any black person who did not surrender on command. All Southern states had laws that prevented blacks from testifying in court against whites, so patrollers could terrorize black families without fear of punishment.

> **Slave catchers presented the greatest danger to runaways. Unlike patrollers, who were local farmers, the slave catchers were professional human hunters who used dogs to track a runaway's scent.**

Mary Reynolds grew up a slave in Louisiana. She recalled going to a prayer meeting in the woods one night with her parents and sister, a prohibited activity. When the family was returning to the plantation, Mary heard the dogs baying and the sound of horse hooves on the road. She said, "Maw, its them . . . hounds and they'll eat us up." Her mother and father told Mary and her sister to stand alongside a fence post and not move. The parents ran into the woods to distract the patrollers.

Mary and her sister stood there, "holdin' hands, shakin' so we can hardly stand. We hears the hounds come nearer, but we don't move. They goes after paw and maw . . ." Luckily, her parents made it inside their cabin before the dogs reached them, and Mary and her sister made it home safely, too.

B Stands for Bloodhound

Sometimes, if not stopped by their owner, dog packs would tear a fugitive to pieces. This is part of the poem, "The Gospel of Slavery: A Primer of Freedom," printed in 1864. Who is the beast according to this poem?

B Stands for Bloodhound
On merciless fangs
The Slaveholder feels that his "property" hangs
And the dog and the master are hot on the track,
To torture or bring the black fugitive back.
The weak has but fled from the hand of the strong,
Asserting the right and resisting the wrong,
While he who exults in a skin that is white,
A Bloodhound employs in asserting his might.
—O chivalry-layman and dogmatist-priest,
Say, which is the monster—the man or the beast?

DISGUISE AND DECEPTION

While the Fugitive Slave Law of 1850 made it harder to escape slavery, fugitives and their allies on the Underground Railroad changed their tactics to better avoid capture. Conductors and runaways became masters of disguise. They invented many methods of escape and built hard-to-find hiding places. When these strategies failed, fugitives fought back, taking their freedom by force.

Hiding in plain sight was the way William and Ellen Craft escaped slavery in the Deep South. In 1848, Ellen, a fair-skinned woman, disguised herself as an injured, rich male planter who was headed north for medical treatment.

WORDS TO KNOW

She bandaged her face to muffle her voice and kept her right arm in a sling so she would not be expected to sign anything. The sling was a critical part of the disguise because Ellen was **illiterate**, and a rich man from the planting elite would certainly know how to write. Ellen's husband, William, pretended to be her slave. The couple traveled all the way from Georgia to Massachusetts and no one questioned their disguise.

SAFE SIGNS

Fugitives often had to make their own way from station to station. Conductors sometimes used signals to communicate. Harriet Tubman used the hoot of an owl and John Rankin left a lantern burning in his window to show that his house was a refuge. Runaways always had to be careful of whom they trusted.

Slave catchers sometimes hired free blacks to pose as fugitives in order to trap an Underground Railroad agent. Therefore, when a conductor or fugitive knocked on the door of a safe house, the stationmaster used a code to determine if the runaway was really who he claimed to be. When the stationmaster asked, "Who is it?" the conductor replied, "The friend of a friend."

Arnold Gragston, an enslaved man who lived on the Kentucky side of the Ohio River, used a code phrase in his work helping slaves. Gragston's owner let him move about without a lot of restriction. He worked for four years helping fugitive slaves cross the river to John Rankin's house.

Three or four times a month, on moonless nights, Gragston arranged to meet fugitives on the Kentucky shore. He would ask a single question: "What you say?" Out of the darkness would come the one-word reply: "Menare." This password proved that these fugitives were legitimate and not a trap. *Menare* is the Italian word for "lead."

This was what agents on the Underground Railroad had pledged their lives to do—lead people to freedom.

One night in 1863, someone spotted him at work, and Gragston rowed across the river for the last time to escape the consequences. Arnold Gragston lived out the rest of his life as a free man in Detroit.

SAFE PLACES

Boxes, barrels, wagon beds, and crawl spaces—these were some of the places fugitive slaves hid themselves. The more ingenuous the hiding spot, the more likely the runaway could avoid detection.

In 1849, Samuel Smith packed his friend Henry Brown into a box. Brown weighed 200 pounds and was 5 feet, 8 inches tall. The box was 3 feet long, 2 feet wide, and just over 2 feet deep. Smith drilled three air holes in the box, addressed it to the Philadelphia Antislavery Society, and delivered Brown to the railway express office in Richmond, Virginia.

After traveling for 27 hours by wagon, train, and steamer, Brown was delivered to Underground Railroad agents who waited for him at the Antislavery Society office. As one man pried open the box, several others watched, afraid they would find a corpse.

Instead, Brown stood up on shaky legs, extended his hand, and said, "How do you do, gentlemen?" What physical challenges would Brown have encountered during the hours he spent in the box? What emotional challenges?

Brown was not the only enslaved person to use extreme measures to reach freedom. In 1835, Harriet Jacobs ran from her sexually abusive master.

The resurrection of Henry Brown at Philadelphia (Library of Congress)

However, she had only the help of a couple relatives, not the Underground Railroad.

Unable to find a safe way out of Edenton, North Carolina, Jacobs hid in a crawl space in her grandmother's cabin. At its peak, the space was only 4 feet high. Mice ran over Harriet's bed at night. When it rained, water leaked in and soaked her bed and clothes. Harriet Jacobs spent seven years in that crawl space before a friend found a ship captain willing to take her to Philadelphia. The length of Harriet's stay shows how difficult it was for slaves to escape when they did not have the assistance of Underground Railroad agents. What else does it show?

The entire community of Oberlin, Ohio, was a station on the Underground Railroad. Oberlin College was founded in 1833, and two years later, the school took a radical step—it began admitting nonwhite students. That same year, the Oberlin Anti-Slavery Society was formed, dedicated to the immediate emancipation of slaves.

The Underground Railroad Goes Underground

One of the only places where the Underground Railroad was actually underground can be seen at the Milton House Museum in southern Wisconsin. The house was built in 1844 by Joseph Goodrich to serve as a stagecoach inn. Goodrich was an abolitionist, and when he built the inn, he also constructed a 44-foot tunnel that led from the inn's cellar to a log cabin behind the house. Fugitive slaves hid in the cellar and used the tunnel to leave the inn quickly when necessary.

stronghold: an area where most people have the same beliefs and values.

conscience: a person's beliefs about what is morally right.

WORDS TO KNOW

By the late 1850s, the town had a black population of 344 people, including 28 fugitive slaves. African Americans worked as saddle makers, masons, and carpenters. They farmed, ran businesses, and attended the college.

Many of these individuals knew the horror of slavery from personal experience, and they worked alongside white abolitionists to shelter fugitives.

The 1858 kidnapping of John Price reveals how the network operated in Oberlin. Price escaped from slavery in Kentucky in the mid-1850s. He had been living in Oberlin for two years when slave catchers arrived in 1858. The two hunters, Anderson Jennings and Richard Mitchell, knew the town was an abolitionist **stronghold**, so they wanted to nab Price quickly and quietly.

The pair conspired with pro-slavery locals to lure Price out of town with the promise of work. Mitchell, accompanied by a federal marshal, weapons, and a warrant, forced Price into a carriage and drove him to the nearby town of Wellington to catch the southbound train to Kentucky.

News of the kidnapping spread through Oberlin. White and black citizens raced to Wellington. Soon, almost 500 men crowded the street in front of the hotel where Price was being held. They shouted at the slave catchers to release him, claiming the kidnapping was illegal. Just then, the train rolled into town.

DID YOU KNOW?

The abolitionist town of Oberlin, Ohio, had a black lawyer named John Mercer Langston.

Price escaped in the chaos. The crowd paraded back to Oberlin in jubilation and held a bonfire in the town square. Price was sheltered in the home of an Oberlin professor until it was safe enough to move him out of town. Eventually, the man reached Canada and freedom.

Prosecutors pressed charges against some of the men who had been present when Price escaped from the hotel. During the trial, defense lawyers claimed the defendants were following a law that was "higher" than the Fugitive Slave Law—their **conscience**.

Eventually, Simeon Bushnell and Charles Langston were convicted. Langston boldly addressed the court, saying every man "had a right to his liberty under the laws of God."

Bushnell received a 60-day jail sentence, but the judge was so moved by Langston's words that he gave him only 20 days in jail—far shorter than the six months allowed by the law.

FIGHTING BACK

Some Underground Railroad agents used force to protect fugitives. On September 11, 1851, in Christiana, Pennsylvania, a battle broke out between pro-slavery and anti-slavery forces that Frederick Douglass labeled "Freedom's Battle."

Three Maryland slaves escaped from owner Edward Gorsuch and sought shelter in Lancaster County, Pennsylvania. An informant told Gorsuch where he could find the men. Gorsuch got the necessary warrants from Philadelphia officials and rounded up a **posse** that included federal marshal Henry Kline.

A "Special Secret Committee" in Philadelphia had been trailing Kline. They sent word to the black population of Lancaster that slave catchers were on the way. The fugitives were hiding in the house of John Parker, who had weapons and was ready to fight.

DID YOU KNOW? John Parker was a fugitive who had escaped slavery in 1839.

Henry Kline and Edward Gorsuch barged into the house at dawn on September 11. They were met by Parker and the other fugitives, plus a crowd of friends and neighbors, all of whom attacked Kline and Gorsuch with rifles, clubs, and scythes. Gorsuch was killed and Kline fled. Afterward, the fugitives and the Parker family fled to Canada. Although the federal government charged some members of the crowd with treason and murder, a jury found them innocent on all counts.

A HIGH PRICE

Not all runaways escaped. Those who were recaptured paid a terrible price. Whites who aided runaways could be fined or jailed, but owners took blood and flesh from their slaves as punishment.

Most owners believed physical pain discouraged future escape attempts. Fugitives were whipped, paddled, beaten, branded, and sometimes had their ears sliced off. If the slave was considered likely to run again, he was usually sold to a plantation in the Deep South.

As a teenager, Moses Roper was determined to escape his owner, John Gooch. Gooch was just as determined to break Roper's spirit. After one failed attempt to flee, Gooch lashed Roper 500 times on his bare back and chained him in a pen where he lay all night on a dirt floor. The next morning, Gooch tied Roper to a heavy plow, forcing him to drag it to the cotton field like an ox.

After another escape attempt, Gooch bent 20-pound iron bars around Roper's feet and hung him from his wrists. A third escape resulted in Gooch putting Roper's hand in a vice and squeezing until all Roper's fingernails peeled off. Then Gooch beat off Roper's toenails with a hammer. Still, Roper tried to run, so Gooch eventually sold him.

Moses Roper finally escaped from slavery in 1835 and moved to England.

A bold and desperate courage was required to attempt escape. Slavery was brutal, so it makes sense that enslaved people would risk everything to run. But what motivated agents on the Underground Railroad to take the chances they did? In the next chapter, you will meet conductors and stationmasters, some famous and others unknown. These men and women shared one trait—they were willing to sacrifice their lives and livelihoods for the human rights of others.

ESSENTIAL QUESTION

Now it's time to consider and discuss the Essential Question: Why would slaves risk the dangers of escape to gain their freedom?

ADVERTISEMENT TRANSFORMATION

When enslaved people ran away, owners posted notices in the newspapers and on broadsides. Sometimes, the qualities that an owner described as negative in the advertisement were actually strengths that could help the fugitive.

(PS)

$5 REWARD.

RUNAWAY, since the 29th of January 1851, the negro ANTOINE, alias WILLIAM, a well known journeyman baker, about 40 years of age, 5 feet 7 or 8 inches tall, yellowish complexion, strong constitution, large head, big nose, thick lips, large flat feet, a large burnt scar on the chest, a piece of one ear bitten off, and speaking English and French.

Any person who will give shelter to that negro, either on land or on board of any ship, will be sued according to the law.

The above reward will be given to any person who will bring back said slave to his master, No. 102, Orleans street, or will lodge him in any of the jails in New Orleans or Lafayette, where it is said his wife is now residing.   f4, 6, 3pw.

(*The Louisiana Courier*, February 4, 1851)

Analyze the advertisement, above, posted in 1851 for a runaway slave.

What does this ad tell you about the appearance, character, and skills of this fugitive slave? How might these characteristics hurt the slave's ability to avoid recapture? How might these characteristics help the slave remain free? What does this ad reveal about the kind of person who placed the ad?

Rewrite this ad to make it positive. Imagine the owner is writing a letter to recommend this slave for a job. How can you turn the qualities that the writer identifies as flaws into strengths?

ACTIVITY

WOULD YOU BREAK THE LAW?

People involved in the Underground Railroad were technically criminals. They broke federal and state laws. They **justified** their actions because they believed slavery was evil, so any law that supported slavery was also evil. Refusing to obey a law that you believe is morally wrong is called **civil disobedience**. American history is full of examples of times when civil disobedience led to social change.

Read each of the following examples of students who engaged in civil disobedience and were punished by their school districts. Whose actions do you agree with in each scenario—the students' or the school administrators'?

* The United States is fighting in World War II. Some students who are Jehovah's Witnesses refuse to salute the flag and recite the "Pledge of Allegiance" because it violates their religious belief. The school expels the students.

* The United States is engaged in the Vietnam War. Some students come to school wearing black armbands to show their opposition to the war. The school district has a policy that bans such armbands because they "disrupt the educational environment." The children are suspended from school.

* There is a protest march through town on a school day by a group protesting government cuts to educational programs. A group of students skips class to attend the march. The school district gives the students unexcused absences.

* Hundreds of high school students walk out of school in protest after the school board decides to eliminate the teaching of civil disobedience from the history curriculum because it fosters a negative image of the United States. Students are given unexcused absences for the time they miss school.

EXPLORE MORE: Most of these cases were appealed and traveled through the judicial system. Research civil disobedience in American schools to see if you can find any of the final verdicts.

WORDS TO KNOW

justify: to prove or show evidence that something is right.

civil disobedience: nonviolent protest, refusing to obey a law because it violates one's moral beliefs.

THE ECONOMICS OF SLAVERY

In 1825, Captain John Anderson bought 100 acres in Kentucky and became a peddler of flesh. He made annual trips to slave auctions in Natchez, Mississippi, and New Orleans, Louisiana, and bought slaves from local farmers. This was a profitable business. From 1832 to 1834, Anderson made $50,000. Today, that is equivalent to $1.25 million. Below is a letter Anderson wrote in 1832.

Letter from John Anderson:

November 24, 1832

Dear Friend,

May next there should not be any more negroes brought to the state for sale and I think in the spring they will be brisk. Negroe men is worth in market at this time from five hundred and fifty to $650 and field women from $400 to $425. I have sold 13 and had 3 to dye with collera, 2 men that cost $900 one child worth $100. The 16 cost $5955 and the 13 I sold brought me $7640 . . . .

I want you to find out and purchaise all the negroes you can of a sertain description: men and boys from 12 to 25 years old and girls from 12 to 20 and noe children. Don't give more than $400 to $450 for men from 17 to 25 years, sound in body and mine, and likely boys from $250 to $350, girls from 15 to 20 $300-$325 and yonger . . . .

Yours,
John W. Anderson

ACTIVITY

When Anderson died, he owned 16 male slaves and 16 female slaves. Use the information in Anderson's letter to complete the following math problems.

* What was the average price for adult male slaves? What was the average price of field women?

* Assume that Anderson paid $300 for each male slave. If he sold them at the average price you figured out, what is the net profit that Anderson made on his male slaves?

* Assume that Anderson paid $200 for each female slave. If he sold them at the average price you figured out, what is the net profit that Anderson made on his female slaves?

* How much money did Anderson lose at the death of the three slaves he mentions in the first paragraph of his letter?

* Calculate Anderson's net profits made on all his slaves. (Don't forget to factor in the loss of the three slaves.)

EXPLORE MORE: The value of the dollar in 1834 is not the same as the value of the dollar today. Inflation has caused the prices of things to increase over time. Take the number you calculated of Anderson's net profits and multiply it by a **conversion rate** of 25. This is roughly how much money Anderson made in modern dollars. Would you consider Anderson to have been a wealthy man? Why or why not?

WORDS TO KNOW

conversion rate: a number used to calculate what value money from an earlier time in history has in today's economy.

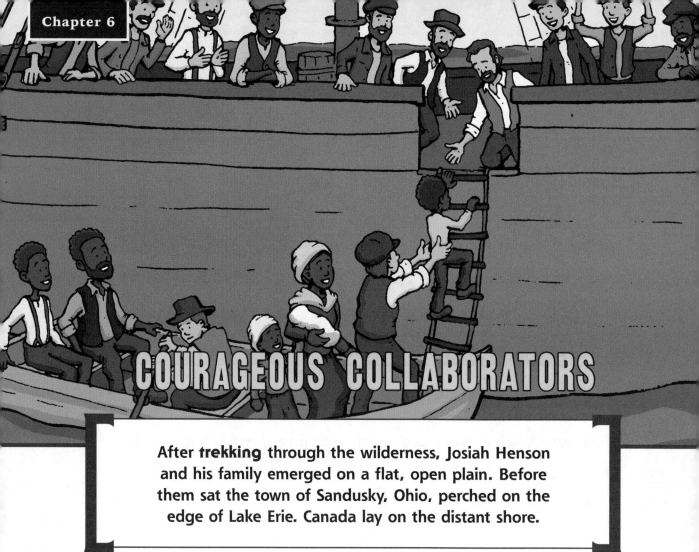

Chapter 6

COURAGEOUS COLLABORATORS

After trekking through the wilderness, Josiah Henson and his family emerged on a flat, open plain. Before them sat the town of Sandusky, Ohio, perched on the edge of Lake Erie. Canada lay on the distant shore.

A group of men were moving back and forth between a building and the lakeshore. After hiding his family behind some bushes, Josiah approached the men. They hired him on the spot to help load cargo on ships. As Josiah worked alongside another African American man, he asked for information about how to get to Canada. The man, realizing Josiah was a runaway, introduced him to the captain, who offered to take him to Buffalo, New York, where the ship was headed.

? ESSENTIAL QUESTION

Why did people help runaway slaves if it was so dangerous?

trek: to walk for a long distance.

schooner: a sailing ship with two masts.

WORDS TO KNOW

The captain said it was too dangerous to load the Hensons on the **schooner** in daylight. Slave hunters watched the docks. The captain offered to sail his ship to a nearby island, weigh anchor, and send a boat back for the Hensons when night fell.

That evening, the family waited in hiding as the ship sailed away. Suddenly, the schooner swung around, sails flapping in the wind, and a small boat was lowered into the water from the side of the ship. Ten minutes later, the boat reached the shore. Three sailors jumped out to help the Hensons board, and then quickly and quietly they rowed the boat out to meet the schooner. Josiah recalled that when his family finally climbed aboard the schooner, they were greeted with "three hearty cheers."

Josiah Henson did not make his journey to freedom alone. Allies along the way assisted him. Some, such as the Native Americans he encountered in the wilderness, were just kind strangers. But others were agents of the Underground Railroad, committed to the cause of freedom.

DID YOU KNOW?

By 1860, the dollar value of the American slaves was worth more than all America's banks, railroads, and manufacturing businesses combined.

CONDUCTORS

Most of the Underground Railroad operated above the Mason-Dixon Line. This boundary between Pennsylvania and Maryland marked the line between slave states and free states. Fugitives were largely on their own until they reached this border or the Ohio River. However, a handful of brave conductors traveled into the South to lead slaves to freedom.

hallucination:
seeing, hearing, or smelling something that seems real but is usually caused by illness or a drug.

expedition: a journey with a specific purpose.

WORDS TO KNOW

Harriet Tubman was a tiny woman with a core of steel. Her childhood as a slave on a Maryland plantation was brutal. She never got enough to eat and sometimes had to fight the hogs for their mash.

The fear of being sold away from her parents and eight siblings was constant.

When Tubman was a teenager, an event changed her life, physically and spiritually. Tubman and the plantation cook had gone to a local store one evening to buy goods for the house. A slave owned by another plantation had left work without permission and was also at the store. His overseer found him and was enraged. The overseer picked up a 2-pound weight from the counter and threw it at the slave. His aim was off. The weight hit Tubman so hard it broke her skull and drove a piece of her shawl into her head.

Tubman recovered slowly, but not completely. For the rest of her life, she suffered from episodes where she would suddenly fall asleep without warning. She also experienced visions, often seeing bright lights and hearing music or screaming.

Today, historians believe Tubman suffered brain damage from the blow to her head. But she was a deeply religious woman and she interpreted these **hallucinations** as messages from God.

In 1849, Tubman discovered she was about to be sold, so she decided to run. She dared not tell her mother her plans. Some of Tubman's siblings had already been sold and her mother's "cries and groans" at the loss of another child could give Tubman away. That night, Tubman made her escape.

Tubman traveled by night, guided by the North Star, and eventually reached Pennsylvania. She was overjoyed, but also lonely. "I was free, but there was no one to welcome me to this land of freedom. I was a stranger in a strange land."

For the next decade, she worked as a maid and cook in Philadelphia, saving every cent to fund **expeditions** back to Maryland. In December 1854, Tubman slipped into the state to rescue three of her brothers scheduled to be sold at auction the day after Christmas. On Christmas morning, Tubman, her three brothers, and three other slaves hunkered in the corncrib outside their parents' cabin waiting for darkness so they could flee.

Tubman had not seen her mother for five years. Now, through the chinks in the corncrib walls, she watched her mother step out of her cabin, look down the empty road, and sigh. She was expecting her sons for Christmas dinner. They would never show up.

Myth Buster: Reward Offered

There is a myth that Southerners were so enraged about the number of slaves Harriet Tubman helped escape they put a $40,000 reward on her. This is false. Only several years after Tubman began rescuing family members did slave holders along the East Coast realize that someone must be aiding them. However, they never suspected Tubman.

WORDS TO KNOW

compile: to organize together into a single publication.

poverty: to be poor.

plague: to cause serious problems or irritation.

Harriet Tubman refused to leave any loved one in bondage. She made 13 trips south and guided between 70 to 80 slaves to freedom, including her elderly parents. She helped another 50 people by providing directions on how to escape. Tubman was called "Moses," after the figure in the Bible who led the Hebrew people out of slavery in Egypt.

Tubman conducted her rescue missions in the winter because the nights were longer and darkness cloaked the fugitives. She met runaways in cemeteries because it was natural for slaves to gather in groups in such a place. She often disguised herself as an elderly man or woman.

She died at age 91, a free woman surrounded by friends and family she had helped free. There were other conductors who traveled into slave states and met a more tragic fate.

DID YOU KNOW?

Harriet Tubman often carried a book, even though she was illiterate. The book was part of her costume.

PS

William Still: Record Keeper

William Still was born free in New Jersey and moved to Philadelphia as an adult. Ambitious and hardworking, he was hired as a clerk for the Pennsylvania Anti-Slavery Society in 1847. By night, he aided fugitives, about 15 each month. He interviewed everyone who came to him, refusing to allow the fugitives' stories to disappear into the dust of history. Still said, "The heroism and desperate struggle that many of our people had to endure should be kept green in the memory . . . ." Following the Civil War, Still **compiled** these interviews into a book. *The Underground Railroad: The Record* is the most complete, detailed account of this secret network. You can read it at this website.

deila dickinson william still text 🔍

STOP SLAVE STEALERS

Seth Concklin grew up in **poverty** in New York. His own struggles made him sympathetic to other people's misery. One day, Concklin read an interview written by William Still, a free black man who worked for the Pennsylvania Anti-Slavery Society and directed the city's Vigilance Committee. Still had interviewed a former slave named Peter Friedman. When Friedman was six, he was sold away from his parents and siblings. It took him 40 years, but he managed to save up $500 to buy his freedom. However, Friedman could not afford to purchase his wife and three children.

Leaving them in Alabama, he came to Philadelphia to raise the money to buy his family. During the course of their interview, Still realized that Peter Friedman was his long-lost brother. Their mother had escaped from slavery years earlier and married a free man. That man was William Still's father.

Concklin was deeply moved by Peter Friedman's story and volunteered to rescue his family.

It was an effort **plagued** with risk. Alabama was in the Deep South, far from any Underground Railroad connections, but Concklin made the trip safely and found Friedman's wife and children. His plan was to bring the fugitives north by steamboat disguised as a master and his slaves. However, the steamboat was late and Conklin's plans fell apart.

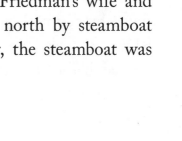

Afraid to wait at the dock any longer, Concklin purchased a skiff and rowed upriver for seven days and seven nights. They made it as far as Vincennes, Indiana, before someone questioned why Concklin was traveling with the blacks. Terrified, the fugitives and Concklin provided different stories. The fugitive slaves were jailed, but Concklin was not. He could have escaped with his life, but he went to the jail to help the Friedmans. This was a tragic mistake.

The Friedmans were returned to slavery, and Seth Concklin's dead body was found the next day washed up on the bank of the river.

Conductors who operated in free states also faced risks, especially those working along the border with the South. John Parker was born a slave. After many failed efforts to flee, he saved enough money to buy his freedom and he moved to Ripley, Ohio. Parker was a successful iron forger and entrepreneur, and at night he conducted fugitives across the Ohio River.

DID YOU KNOW?

John Parker made his first attempt to escape at age 10.

One night, Parker received word that a group of fugitives from central Kentucky was hiding in the woods about 20 miles from the river. Parker put a pair of pistols in his pockets and a knife in his belt and volunteered to aid the runaways. His collaborators in Ripley promised to have a boat waiting to pick the group up after nightfall.

Parker found eight male and two female fugitives deep in the Kentucky woods. The forest was so thick that the group could travel by day without detection. As a result, they reached the Ohio River at dusk. No boat was waiting for them because they had arrived before the appointed time.

Suddenly, the howl of dogs cut through the air. Slave catchers were close. Parker raced along the river's edge, hoping someone had left a vessel in the weeds. He was in luck. A small skiff lay in the tall grass. But if 11 people tried to cram into the boat, it would sink. Parker had no choice but to abandon two men on the shore. One of the women in the boat began to cry. Her husband was being left behind. Without a word, a single man on the boat climbed out, giving his spot to the husband.

As Parker's boat neared the Ohio shore, he heard shouts and saw lights where the two fugitives had been standing. Parker understood what this meant. ". . . The poor fellow[s] had been captured in sight of the promised land." He'd had to make a split-second decision about who he could bring to freedom and who he must leave behind.

The strain on conductors was so great that few conductors could work more than a decade before their nerves gave out.

STATIONMASTERS

After a conductor led fugitives to a station on the Underground Railroad, the stationmaster took over. Stationmasters were in charge of feeding, clothing, sheltering, and protecting the runaways until they were moved down the line. Fugitives might stay at a station for a couple of hours or a couple of weeks.

oppression: an unjust or cruel use of authority and power.

WORDS TO KNOW

Detroit was a major gateway to Canada. A collection of free blacks served as stationmasters for this critical depot. The Colored Vigilant Committee worked to improve the status of free blacks in the city. They fought for better schools, the right to vote, and the abolition of slavery. Many members of this committee were also active in the city's Underground Railroad.

William Lambert (1817–1890) coordinated many of the Underground Railroad operations in the city. Born free in New Jersey, he moved to Detroit as a young man, opened a tailor shop, and became wealthy.

Lambert used his money to finance rescue efforts for those escaping slavery.

Lambert founded a secret society called the African American Mysteries Order of the Men of **Oppression**. George DeBaptiste, who had worked as part of the Underground Railroad in Indiana before moving to Michigan, was another member of this group. These men, almost all African Americans, worked to shelter and transport slaves escaping across the Detroit River toward freedom.

Only members of the order knew the elaborate system of secret passwords and handshakes. With this system, agents could detect traps set by slave catchers.

Stockholders

Gerrit Smith, heir to a fur-trading fortune, donated the modern equivalent of $1 billion to buy and free enslaved families. He also financed rescue efforts and funded Frederick Douglass's abolitionist newspaper, *The North Star*. Smith and other rich abolitionists who donated funds to keep the network functioning were known as stockholders of the Underground Railroad.

Agents selected to travel south to rescue fugitives had to swear a solemn oath not to take anyone into their confidences unless the person was trustworthy. Those who broke this oath were considered traitors. It is unknown how many slaves were helped by this order, but certainly there were many.

WOMEN'S WORK

Women did much of the work that kept the Underground Railroad running smoothly. When runaways arrived at the home of Frederick Douglass in Rochester, New York, or Levi Coffin in Cincinnati,

Ohio, it was their wives, Anna Douglass and Catherine Coffin, who made up the beds and cooked the food.

Women sewed quilts and clothing for fugitives, nursed them when they were ill, and tended to their frightened children. They circulated anti-slavery petitions and sold homemade pies and jams to raise money to fund rescue efforts. The Cleveland, Ohio, vigilance committee had only nine members, and four of them were women.

The knowledge that they were helping fugitives reach freedom inspired agents on the Underground Railroad to continue their dangerous work. In the next chapter, you will explore how former slaves worked to carve out lives as free people—some in Canada and others in the United States after the North and the South had fought a bloody civil war.

ESSENTIAL QUESTION

Now it's time to consider and discuss the Essential Question: Why did people help runaway slaves if it was so dangerous?

YOU CAN TAKE THIS HERO TO THE BANK

The Treasury Department plans to put Harriet Tubman on the $20 bill. She will be the first African American woman, and only the third woman, to appear on American paper money. The bills will come out in the year 2020 to mark the 100-year anniversary of all women gaining the right to vote in the United States.

Design your own $20 bill with symbols, illustrations, and words that communicate the role of Harriet Tubman in American history.

✱ What phrases might be included on the bill?

Research online and find images of Harriet Tubman.

✱ Which picture should the government use on the bill? Why?

✱ Are there any images that symbolize the work she did on the Underground Railroad?

EXPLORE MORE:
Harriet Tubman will replace President Andrew Jackson on the $20 bill. He was put on the bill in 1928, but historians are not sure why. There is little documentation about that decision made by the Treasury Department. Research President Jackson's life. Does he deserve to keep his spot on the $20 bill or is Harriet Tubman a better model of an American hero?

THROUGH THEIR EYES

One of the ways historians try to understand the past is to consider the world through the eyes of people who lived at a certain time. In this activity, you will try to create the mindset of a fugitive slave.

Go to this link to find the text of a book of fugitive interviews compiled by William Still. The second link brings you to a drawing found in another version of the book.

archive william still underground railroad 🔍

twenty-eight fugitives escaping 🔍

Read a few of the interviews.
Then study the drawing. Choose one of the fugitives illustrated. Write an interior monologue from their point of view, weaving in the information you read in the interviews. An interior monologue is a piece of writing that expresses a character's innermost thoughts from his or her point of view.

★ What is this character most afraid of? What are his or her worries?

★ What gives this character hope?

★ Does this character feel strong? Weak? Hopeful?

★ What made you choose this character?

DID YOU KNOW?

There was no director or president in all the decades the Underground Railroad was in operation. It was a **grassroots** organization. The power to make decisions rested in the hands of ordinary men and women.

EXPLORE MORE: What insights can writing from the point of view of a historic person give you that traditional essay writing cannot? What are the problems of this kind of creative historical writing?

WORDS TO KNOW

grassroots: an organization made up of many ordinary people.

LET'S SHAKE ON IT

The Order of the Men of Oppression taught a secret handshake to runaways. According to William Lambert, ". . . The sign was pulling the knuckle of the right forefinger over the knuckle of the same finger of the left hand. The answer was to reverse the fingers as described."

Are you a member of a special group, such as a club, sports team, or musical group? Create a special greeting for just group members.

If you want your membership to be secret, design a greeting that will not be obvious to an outsider. The greeting does not have to involve your hands. You could tug on an earlobe or tap your elbow or hop on one leg.

Secret Societies

There have been several documented secret societies in world history. The Freemasons, founded in 1717, is one of the oldest known groups. It was founded as a mutual aid society where members came to the assistance of other members. The Skull and Bones is a secret society formed at Yale University in 1832. Today, it seems to function mainly as a social group. The Internet makes it harder to keep the doings of any organization secret today. However, Anonymous is a loosely connected international network of activists who hack government communications and leak them to the public. If this group has a secret handshake, it is probably a digital one.

ACTIVITY

MAP YOUR ROUTE

What route would you choose to travel from slavery to freedom? In this activity, you will plot your journey north.

Do some research at the library and find a map of the United States in the 1850s.

✱ If you were a fugitive running away from slavery in Richmond, Virginia, what would be the safest, quickest route to Montreal in Canada?

✱ What rivers or mountains would you have to cross?

✱ What cities would you travel through?

✱ If you could walk 15 miles a day, how many days would the journey take you?

EXPLORE MORE: What do you predict will be the most dangerous segment of your journey? How can you prepare for this? Are there other routes you can take? Other destinations to choose?

Question and Answer

William Lambert claimed that the questions and answers below were taught to every fugitive his secret order aided. Runaways were expected to be able to answer them correctly in order to get assistance.

› Q. Have you ever been on the railroad?
A. I have been a short distance.

› Q. Where did you start from?
A. The depot.

› Q. Where did you stop?
A. At a place called Safety.

› Q. Have you a brother there? I think I know him.
A. I know you now.

Chapter 7

FREEDOM FOUND

Josiah Henson remembered the moment his life changed forever. On the morning of October 28, 1830, his feet touched the Canadian shore. Josiah threw himself to the ground and rolled in the sand, then rose to his feet and danced. One passerby commented, "He's some crazy fellow." Josiah called back, "Oh no, master. Don't you know? I'm free!" Then he hugged and kissed his wife and children, who were also overjoyed. However, Josiah knew there was not much time for celebration. The family needed a place to live and a way to make a living if freedom was going to live up to their expectations.

THE PROMISED LAND

Fugitives and free blacks had sought refuge in Canada for decades, but after the 1850 Fugitive Slave Act, the trickle of people became a flood. The **province** of Ontario was located between Lake Huron and Lake Erie. It offered several doorways the Underground Railroad could use to enter Canada.

? ESSENTIAL QUESTION

Could slavery have been abolished without the Civil War?

The Canadian border did not stop all slave catchers. Some of them entered Canada and posted reward notices. They approached Canadian employers and tried to buy escaped slaves. Slave holders also went to court, demanding Canada return their property.

The case of Thorton and Ruth Blackburn set the precedent for how the Canadian legal system would react to demands from American citizens and pressure from American politicians.

The Blackburns escaped from Kentucky in 1831 and moved to Detroit. Two years later, they were captured. Underground Railroad operators launched a dramatic rescue. On Sunday, June 16, a crowd of angry, armed blacks gathered near the Detroit jail where the Blackburns were being held in separate cells. Two women begged the sheriff to let them visit Ruth Blackburn one last time. He let them into her cell. The women emerged a short time later, their faces veiled as they wept loudly. When the jailer went to fetch Ruth later, he found one of the visitors in her place.

The next day, Thorton was brought to the door of his jail cell in chains, surrounded by the jailer and sheriff. A crowd of angry blacks greeted them outside the jail. Alarmed by the crowd, the sheriff tried to return Thorton to his cell. Before the sheriff could retreat, a man in the crowd tossed Thorton a gun. Thorton fired into the air, launching the Blackburn Riot of 1833.

extradite: to hand over a person accused of a crime to the country or state where the crime was committed.

vocational: related to skills or training needed for a specific job.

WORDS TO KNOW

While the mob attacked the sheriff, Thorton ran. He made it across the Detroit River into Canada. The entire rescue had been engineered by Detroit's leaders of the Underground Railroad.

The sheriff died from his injuries the following year. Many blacks were arrested after the riot and 10 eventually served jail time. White citizens struck back against African Americans following this event. They attacked blacks in the streets and burned the homes of African Americans. Many blacks sold or abandoned their property and moved to Canada.

United States officials sent notice to Canada demanding the arrest and **extradition** of Thorton Blackburn. They claimed he had started a riot and tried to kill the sheriff. Canadian police arrested Thorton and held him in jail. However, a Canadian court concluded that if Thorton was returned to the United States, even if he was found innocent of charges relating to the riot, he would still be returned to slavery.

> Canadian law prevented extraditing people to a country that imposed harsher penalties then they would get for the same offense in Canada. Thorton and Ruth Blackburn lived out the rest of their lives in Canada as free people.

This case would determine how future runaway disputes between Canada and the United States would be settled. When American slaves crossed the Canadian border, they would not be returned to the United States.

DAWN OF A NEW DAY

Former slaves found freedom in Canada, but not equality. Some white Canadians resented the presence of blacks in their communities. Some provinces prohibited African Americans from buying land, building homes, or attending school. They did have more legal rights in Canada, however, than they ever had in the United States. They could become citizens, vote, and file a lawsuit. Building a new life was hard, despite these new freedoms. The joy of escaping slavery faded as refugees faced poverty and homelessness.

Josiah Henson understood the challenges his former countrymen faced. When the Hensons arrived in Canada, they had one dollar and the clothes on their backs. The family first lived in a run-down hut that had been used as a pigsty. With hard work, Josiah eventually purchased land overlooking the Detroit River. He and some other investors founded Dawn, a community for former slaves.

Dawn revolved around the British American Institute, a school that taught **vocational** skills. Settlers grew wheat, corn, and tobacco and harvested lumber for export to the United States.

Successful Settlement

Dawn was not the only settlement of former slaves. The Buxton settlement, also known as Elgin, was the most successful community. Reverend William King, a white Irishman, purchased 9,000 acres of land two miles from Lake Erie. He divided it into 50-acre plots and black "colonists" could purchase up to 50 acres for $2.50 an acre. The settlers had to clear the land and build a house. By 1857, 800 black settlers had cleared 1,000 acres of land. The town had a sawmill, brickyard, blacksmith and carpenter shops, shoe shops, and grocery stores, as well as several churches and schools. Descendants of these early settlers still live and farm in the region today.

secede: to formally withdraw from a country.

Border States: the slave states of Delaware, Maryland, Missouri, and Kentucky that bordered the North and refused to secede during the Civil War.

chasm: a major separation between two groups.

WORDS TO KNOW

With a gristmill, brickyard, and rope-making factory, Dawn enjoyed success for a short time. But then financial troubles began. When the school closed in 1868, people moved away. Some left for other areas of Canada, but many returned to the United States after slavery was abolished at the end of the Civil War. African Americans wanted to return home.

TORN IN TWO

The sea off Charleston Harbor, South Carolina, was calm the night of April 12, 1861, but the nation was not. Months earlier, South Carolina had **seceded** from the United States and other Southern states quickly followed. Ultimately, 11 slave-owning states joined to form their own independent nation—the Confederate States of America.

The Confederate States of the South were called the Confederacy and the United States of the North were called the Union. The leaders of the Confederacy claimed that Fort Sumter, the fortress on the island in Charleston Harbor, belonged to them. The federal troops inside the fort, representing the Union, must leave, or else.

The new president of the United States, Abraham Lincoln, said the Constitution did not allow any state to secede, and he refused to recognize the Confederacy. Lincoln ordered the troops inside Fort Sumter to stand fast.

At 4:30 on the morning of April 12, the shriek of mortar fire pierced the nervous silence in Charleston. The bombardment of Fort Sumter began, and with it came the Civil War that pitted North against South and decided the fate of slavery. Both sides believed the war would last no more than three months. Both sides were mistaken.

DID YOU KNOW?

Historians do not know exactly how many fugitive slaves escaped to Canada. Census records suggest that in 1861, there were between 20,000 and 23,000 blacks living there.

TO SAVE THE UNION

Although President Lincoln was personally opposed to slavery, in the first months of the war he insisted that his mission was to unify the country, not free the slaves. He told the Confederates that if they laid down their arms, they could keep their slaves. The president did not want to anger the slaveholding **Border States**, fearing they might join the Confederacy.

Fugitive Slaves Were a Cause of War

By the mid-nineteenth century, conflict over slavery had created a **chasm** between the North and South. Confederate states said one of the main reasons they broke from the United States was because Northern communities refused to return their runaway slaves. Abraham Lincoln was a politician from a free state who opposed the spread of slavery. When he was elected president in the fall of 1860, Southerners believed it was only a matter of time before Northern politicians made slavery illegal everywhere.

Enslaved people had no intention of waiting for President Lincoln to change his mind. War created chaos and slaves took advantage of this. The war was barely a month old when Frank Baker, Shepard Mallory, and James Townsend slipped away from a Confederate Army camp located on the Chesapeake Bay in Virginia.

The men had been ordered to dig cannon embankments so the Confederates could fire on Fort Monroe, located on an island in the bay. But one night, they stole a boat, rowed to the Union fort, and asked for refuge. Technically, the Fugitive Slave Law was still in place. Benjamin Butler, the Union general in command of the fort, was legally required to hand the fugitives over to their owners.

But Butler had a better idea. The day after the fugitives escaped, Confederate Major John Cary came to the fort under a white flag and demanded the slaves back. General Butler refused. "I shall hold these Negroes as **contraband** of war," he declared. According to military law, a commander could seize enemy property being used for military purposes.

Since the fugitives had been building Confederate defenses, Butler felt justified in keeping them.

President Lincoln let General Butler's order stand, and word spread throughout slave communities. By June 1861, more than 500 fugitives had sought safety inside Fort Monroe. No one knew if these "contrabands" were slaves or free people. But one thing was certain—the end of slavery had begun.

EMANCIPATION PROCLAMATION

From 1861 through the end of 1862, the conflict between North and South went back and forth in a bloody tug-of-war. Neither side gained any significant ground, and men died by the thousands. Enslaved people in the Confederate states did work that enabled the South to keep fighting. Meanwhile, the fugitives who had escaped wanted to join the Union Army and fight, but were barred from the military. President Lincoln believed "that we had . . . about played our last card, and must change our tactics, or lose the game." The change the president made would alter history.

On January 1, 1863, Lincoln signed the Emancipation Proclamation. This presidential decree declared all slaves in the Confederacy "henceforward shall be free." The Civil War was no longer a conflict to **reunite** the nation as it had been before the war began. It had become a war for the very soul of America.

Would the United States be the land of the free or the land of slavery?

Reaction to the Emancipation Proclamation was mixed. Some abolitionists praised the move while others believed it did not do enough. The proclamation only applied to slaves in the Confederacy. Lincoln did not control this territory and could not enforce the law there. The slaves in the Border States were allowed to keep their slaves. Why did he arrange it this way?

While the proclamation did not free all slaves, it did have something that pleased all African Americans. Blacks, free and fugitive, were finally permitted to join the armed services. They enlisted in droves. By the end of the war, 179,000 blacks would serve in the Army and another 19,000 in the Navy.

TURNING POINT

On July 1, 1863, the small town of Gettysburg, Pennsylvania, erupted in a huge battle. When the guns fell silent three days later, more than 50,000 men lay dead or wounded. This battle shifted the balance of power to the North.

For the next year and a half, the Confederate Army fought a retreating action, slowly moving farther south with each battle.

An 1864 painting by Francis Bicknell Carpenter of President Lincoln presenting the Emancipation Proclamation to his cabinet

As Union troops pursued the Confederate Army, slaves fled the fields and farms. The Union Army organized large camps to provide food and shelter to these refugees. No one was sure what the status of these people would be after the war. The Emancipation Proclamation said slaves in the Confederacy were free, but was it legal for the president to single-handedly take away valuable property from thousands of Southerners?

What about the tens of thousands of slaves in the Border States who had not been freed by the proclamation? Would they remain slaves if the North won the war?

President Lincoln and abolitionist leaders knew the only way to permanently eliminate slavery everywhere was for Congress to amend the Constitution. As the war entered its final days, Lincoln used all his powers of persuasion to convince legislators to pass an amendment to abolish slavery.

Death and desertion shrank the Confederate Army. In early April 1865, Union forces trapped Confederate General Robert E. Lee in the town of Appomattox, Virginia. Down to only 9,000 men and with no hope of reinforcements, Lee surrendered on April 9, 1865. The long and bloody Civil War was over.

ratify: to give official approval of something, such as a constitutional amendment.

WORDS TO KNOW

Less than one week later, President Lincoln was dead, shot by an assassin while he attended the theater. African Americans mourned him, afraid of what would happen now that their protector was dead. But abolitionists in Congress did not give up their fight. On December 6, 1865, the 13th Amendment was **ratified**. It abolished slavery throughout the nation and for all time.

With the end of the Civil War, the Underground Railroad was no longer needed. Stationmasters could lock up their safe houses. Conductors could forget their secret passwords. Stockholders could donate their money to other causes. The time had come for African Americans to begin their lives as free men and women.

However, the Underground Railroad did not disappear. In the next chapter, you will explore ways in which this campaign of civil disobedience influenced other movements in American history. In fact, this once-secret network remains a model of resistance for people around the world today.

 ESSENTIAL QUESTION

Now it's time to consider and discuss the Essential Question: Could slavery have been abolished without the Civil War?

Amendments

The 13th Amendment was not the only change to the Constitution following the Civil War. The 14th Amendment granted citizenship to African Americans and guaranteed equal protection under the law to all Americans. The 15th Amendment gave male citizens the right to vote, regardless of their skin color or whether they had previously been slaves. What about women? It wasn't until the 19th Amendment was ratified in 1920 that American women were granted the right to vote.

DESIGN A NEW HOUSE FOR A NEW LIFE

IDEAS FOR SUPPLIES

building materials (cardboard, poster board, sticks, straws, rocks, clay, duct tape, or paper clips), weighted objects to simulate heavy snow (coins or metal washers), something to create wind (such as a blow dryer or fan)

The climate is much warmer in the American South than in Canada. African American refugees had much to adjust to, but the long, cold winters of Canada were particularly challenging. In this activity, you will design a house to withstand the snows of Canada, which could rise up to 6 to 10 feet every winter.

Brainstorm some features your house will need to keep out strong wind, rain, and heavy snow. Draw your designs in your notebook. Build a model of your house.

* What building materials will you use to keep your house warm?

* How will you design it?

* How strong do your walls and roof have to be?

* How can you use the natural world around your house for protection?

Test the design and strength of your house by putting weights on the roof. Test the strength of your walls by aiming a blow dryer or fan at your house and turning it on. What changes do you need to make so your house can withstand a freezing climate and the storms of winter?

EXPLORE MORE: Very few slave cabins have survived to the present. To understand how slaves were sheltered, historians rely on the memories of former slaves. Read the descriptions of slave dwellings reported by people such as Mary Prince, Austin Steward, Frederick Douglass, and Jacob Stroyer. Based on their accounts, was slave housing adequate? Would you be comfortable living like these people did? Why or why not?

ACTIVITY

GEOGRAPHY AND POLITICS

President Lincoln was criticized for not freeing all enslaved people with the Emancipation Proclamation. What did Lincoln's freedom plan look like on a map?

"That on the first day of January, in the year of our Lord one thousand eight hundred and sixty-three, all persons held as slaves within any State or designated part of a State, the people whereof shall then be in rebellion against the United States, shall be then, thenceforward, and forever free . . .
Arkansas, Texas, Louisiana, Mississippi, Alabama, Florida, Georgia, South Carolina, North Carolina, and Virginia, (except West Virginia) . . . ."

On a blank map, use colors or symbols to identify where slaves were freed by the Emancipation Proclamation and where they were not. Draw a line to distinguish the Union from the Confederacy. Study your shaded map.

* How did geography influence the political decision Lincoln made when he wrote the Emancipation Proclamation?

* Why did he do this?

EXPLORE MORE: Research the reaction of enslaved people in different parts of the country when they heard the news of the Emancipation Proclamation. Were reactions more positive in some areas compared with others?

FREE	SLAVE
PA	GA
CT	MD
MA	SC
ME	MS
NH	VA
NY	NC
RI	KY
VT	TN
OH	LA
IN	MO
IL	AK
MI	FL
IA	TX
WI	OK Territory
CA	NE Territory
MN	
OR	
KS	

Chapter 8

BEYOND FREEDOM

Just before Josiah Henson boarded the ship that would take him across the Niagara River to the shores of Canada, he vowed, "I'll use my freedom well." And he did. One day a man named James Lightfoot approached Josiah. Lightfoot had escaped slavery in Kentucky, but left behind his entire family. Would Henson rescue them? With that request, Josiah Henson became a conductor on the Underground Railroad, helping people the way others had once helped him.

Josiah Henson lived out the rest of his 93 years in Canada. In 1849, his story was published in *The Life of Josiah Henson, Formerly a Slave*. This inspiring memoir recounted one man's struggle to shape his own destiny.

? ESSENTIAL QUESTION

How has your daily life been influenced by the Underground Railroad?

Reconstruction: the period of time after the Civil War when the United States was reorganized and reunited.

Ku Klux Klan: a terrorist group formed after the Civil War that believed white Christians should hold the power in society.

white supremacy: the racist belief that white people are superior to those of all other races, especially the black race, and should therefore dominate society.

civil rights: the rights of citizens to have political, social, and economic equality.

WORDS TO KNOW

The Underground Railroad helped fugitives such as Henson shed the bonds of slavery, and the Civil War abolished slavery forever. However, the freedom of African Americans was not yet complete because they were far from equal.

THE FAILURE OF RECONSTRUCTION

After the Civil War, during a period called **Reconstruction**, a new world opened up for former slaves. For the first time, they had the legal right to get paid for their work, to marry whomever they chose, to go to school, to cast their vote, and to run for office. In some communities, 90 percent of black citizens voted in the first decade after the war.

However, Southern whites fought hard to regain their old power. By 1877, the former class of wealthy white planters was back in control throughout the former Confederacy. Black codes were put into place to prevent African Americans from voting, serving on juries, testifying against whites, or owning guns and land. Schools and other public places were segregated.

Government of all the People

As the former Confederacy was integrated back into the United States, African American men entered politics. Two served in the U.S. Senate, 14 in the House of Representatives, six were elected as lieutenant governors, and more than 600 held seats in state legislatures.

Ku Klux Klan

Some former Confederate soldiers formed the **Ku Klux Klan** in 1865. The organization believed in **white supremacy** and enforced its beliefs through violence. White hoods and robes disguised the identity of the night-riders, Klansmen who committed violence against blacks. Since then, the Klan has ridden waves of popularity and decline. In the 1920s, 4 million Americans were members. The group grew again during the **civil rights** movement of the 1950s and 1960s. Today, there are Ku Klux Klan groups in 41 states, although their membership is small.

Black neighborhoods were targeted by the Ku Klux Klan, a terrorist organization that still exists today.

The federal government was no help as African Americans saw their rights snatched away. Troops had been in place throughout the former Confederacy to enforce peace, but in 1877, President Rutherford Hayes withdrew

Three Ku Klux Klan members parade through counties in northern Virginia bordering on the District of Columbia

these forces. The rights granted to blacks in the 13th, 14th, and 15th Amendments meant nothing when the government failed to enforce the law.

The failure of the government to protect African Americans meant a different sort of slavery. While a Southern white could no longer physically own a black person, he could pay him lower wages than a white and deny him the right to go to school with whites. Blacks could be prevented from voting, banned from owning land, and killed with little fear of punishment.

One hundred years after the Civil War, African Americans rose up and demanded their fair share of the American dream. They used a campaign of civil disobedience just as bold as the Underground Railroad. Leaders such as Dr. Martin Luther King Jr., Daisy Bates, John Lewis, and Diane Nash organized **boycotts** and marches. Activists held sit-ins and filed lawsuits.

Some racist whites fought back with fire hoses, police dogs, bully clubs, and bullets, but slowly things changed. Schools opened their doors to black students. Employers began to hire black workers. States permitted blacks to vote.

A fairer freedom began to develop for the descendants of former slaves.

MODERN SLAVERY

Frederick Douglass predicted slavery would evolve. He said, "Slavery has been fruitful in giving herself names . . . and it will call itself by yet another name. . . ." Douglass was right. Slavery still brutalizes people in the world today, even in the United States.

Amalia is a young Filipino woman. When she took a job as a housekeeper for a Taiwanese diplomat working in Missouri, she was told her salary would be $1,200 a month for a 40-hour work week. That was a lie.

Amalia's employer took her travel documents and threatened to have her arrested if she disobeyed him. He demanded Amalia work 16 hours a day and only paid her $450 a month. Cameras recorded her every move. Amalia was forbidden to leave the house without supervision. This is what slavery looks like in the twenty-first century.

Sadly, 50 percent of today's victims of slavery are children. Teen girls are sold into **prostitution**. Armies kidnap boys, forcing them into the military. Young children are slaves in brick, carpet, shoe, and shirt factories.

Slavery is illegal under international law, but human traffickers work under the radar of law enforcement.

Many groups exist to combat modern slavery. Organizations such as Free International, the Polaris Project, and Project to End Human Trafficking are staffed by modern abolitionists. These groups lobby for better laws and they operate hotlines to help victims.

A woman gave Amalia the number of a hotline run by an anti-slavery organization. Amalia was terrified to call, fearing she might be arrested. But alone and desperate, she finally called. The person who spoke to Amalia on the phone was a conductor of this modern Underground Railroad. This conductor calmed Amalia's fears, found her shelter, and helped her press charges against her employer.

DID YOU KNOW?

Experts estimate that 20 to 30 million people around the world are victims of modern slavery, often called human trafficking.

LEGACY

The history of the Underground Railroad reveals the best and worst of America. Slavery was the single reason for this secret network. Slavery shaped American culture, and its ghost still lingers today in racist attitudes and actions. The Underground Railroad also spotlights Americans' compassion and sacrifice. Agents of the railroad risked everything to come to the aid of African Americans.

The Underground Railroad began with the actions of a few individuals at the turn of the nineteenth century. Within 50 years, it had transformed into a movement that drew people from all walks of life united by a common goal—to liberate enslaved people. These agents demonstrated that people can work together when they believe in a cause. In this aspect, the Underground Railroad was the United States' first civil rights movement.

The Underground Railroad gave women experience at organizing and leading. They learned how to raise funds, organize events, write persuasively, and speak to large groups. Women needed this training because they had a fight of their own to wage. While not enslaved, prior to the twentieth century, women could not vote. They also could not hold office, serve on juries, enter certain professions, or control their own property.

End Slavery Now

Go to this link to examine modern slavery. What type of jobs are people trapped into? How many people are affected? Click "Photo Galleries" on the sidebar menu. What do the photographs of modern slavery reveal about how slavery has both changed and remained the same throughout history?

slavery today 🔎

In 1848, five white women took the skills they had developed in the abolitionist movement and started a revolution. Elizabeth Cady Stanton, Lucretia Coffin Mott, Martha Coffin Wright, Mary Ann M'Clintock, and Jane Hunt organized the first women's rights convention in Seneca Falls, New York. Delegates to the convention drafted the Declaration of Sentiments, which declared "All men and women were created equal." Their work with the Underground Railroad had awakened in women a desire for their own liberty.

TOWARD RACIAL UNDERSTANDING

Now you know the real history of the Underground Railroad. Midnight rides, secret hiding places, daring escapes—there is drama in this chapter of American history. Enslaved people are the heroes of this tale. Their courage, their determination, and their sacrifice in the pursuit of freedom was the engine of the railroad. Free blacks and abolitionist whites willing to defy the law were the train's wheels moving slaves toward freedom.

The Underground Railroad demonstrated three important lessons: People can free themselves from bondage, the actions of a single person can make a difference in the lives of others, and an evil system can be overturned.

What would the world look like if everyone learned these lessons?

The Underground Railroad was a secret in the nineteenth century. It's not a secret anymore. It's a history of personal courage and moral resistance—not black history or white history. The Underground Railroad is American history. Go spread the word.

ESSENTIAL QUESTION

Now it's time to consider and discuss the Essential Question: How has your daily life been influenced by the Underground Railroad?

FREEDOM CHAIN

What does the word "freedom" mean to you? Does it mean playing video games for as long as you want? Hanging out with friends whenever you want? The right to vote? The right to free speech and to debate with your teachers? People from different cultural backgrounds define freedom in different ways.

Think about the freedoms you enjoy, freedoms that many people in the world may not have. Ask some friends to make their list of freedoms. Together, make a freedom chain to celebrate these liberties.

Enslaved people were shackled with iron chains. What material can you use for a chain to represent freedom instead of oppression? Slave shackles were circular links. What shape will your chain be to demonstrate the liberties you cherish? Slave chains were dark colors like the skin tone that condemned generations of people to bondage. What colors will your chain be and what do these colors represent to you?

Stay up late
Read any book I want
Get a job
Go to friend's house
Eat cereal for dinner

MAKE YOUR OWN MEMORIAL

The Gateway to Freedom sculpture in Detroit is a memorial to the Underground Railroad. The statues of nine fugitives and a conductor stand on the banks of the Detroit River, looking toward Canada.

A memorial is a form of art designed to remember a person or event. Memorials can be a statue or plaque, a musical concert, even a tree planted in someone's memory. A memorial cannot tell everything about a person or event. Instead, the designer focuses on an important feature or idea to showcase.

In this activity, you will design a memorial to something or someone that you want to remember. The topic of your memorial could be a person or pet that is no longer in your life, it could be a historical person whom you believe is important or a historical event you think should be remembered. In words and images, answer the following questions about the subject of your memorial to help get your creativity flowing.

* What is the name of your subject?
* Why is the subject important to you?
* What activities and setting would the subject be involved in?
* What does this subject look like?
* What would you say to this subject if you could?
* What would you like other people to know about this subject?

Choose the materials and method to make your memorial. You can write a song, sculpt a statue, paint a picture, or something else!

Create a draft of your memorial design on paper. Revise and improve this and then make a final version of your memorial.

EXPLORE MORE: Put your memorial where other people can view it. Develop a way to get viewer feedback. What kinds of emotions does your memorial fuel in your audience? After they are done viewing it, what do they understand about the subject you have memorialized? Have you achieved your purpose?

abolish: to completely do away with something.

abolitionist: someone who believed that slavery should be abolished, or ended.

abruptly: all of a sudden.

ambitious: having a strong desire to become successful.

amendment: a correction, addition, or change to the U.S. Constitution.

appeal: a legal procedure in which a case is brought before a higher court in order for it to review the decision made by a lower court.

arsenal: a place where weapons and military equipment are stored.

auction: a public sale of property to the highest bidder.

auction block: the platform from which an auctioneer sells goods to a crowd of buyers.

bluff: a high, steep bank.

bondage: another word for slavery.

Border States: the slave states of Delaware, Maryland, Missouri, and Kentucky that bordered the North and refused to secede during the Civil War.

boycott: to stop buying a product or using a service as a way to protest something.

broadside: an advertisement or public notice printed on a large piece of paper and displayed for public viewing.

catalyst: an event that causes a change.

cede: to give up power over a territory to another country.

chasm: a major separation between two groups.

civil disobedience: nonviolent protest, refusing to obey a law because it violates one's moral beliefs.

civilization: a community of people that is advanced in art, science, and government.

civil rights: the rights of citizens to have political, social, and economic equality.

coffle: a line of slaves fastened together.

collaborators: people who work together in order to achieve a goal.

colony: an area that is controlled by or belongs to another country.

commissioner: an official in charge of a government department.

compile: to organize together into a single publication.

congregation: the people who regularly attend a church.

conscience: a person's beliefs about what is morally right.

consent: to agree.

constitution: the basic principles and laws of a nation.

contagion: the spreading of a disease.

contraband: something that it is forbidden to possess.

conversion rate: a number used to calculate what value money from an earlier time in history has in today's economy.

convert: to change.

creditor: someone who is owed money.

cutlass: a short sword with a curved blade.

Deep South: a region of the Southeastern United States that includes the states of Alabama, Georgia, Louisiana, Mississippi, North Carolina, and South Carolina.

defiance: bold disobedience.

delegate: a person sent to a meeting as a representative of a larger group of people or a specific area of the country.

descendant: a person related to someone who lived in the past.

distinct: clearly different.

document: to record.

documentation: a written record of something.

eavesdrop: to listen in on someone else's conversation.

emancipate: to legally free someone.

embed: to put something firmly inside of something else.

enslave: to make someone a slave.

equivocate: to conceal your true opinion.

expedition: a journey with a specific purpose.

extradite: to hand over a person accused of a crime to the country or state where the crime was committed.

fanatic: a person who is wildly enthusiastic or obsessed about only one thing.

fatigue: being very tired.

flog: to beat or whip someone.

free soilers: people who opposed the spread of slavery into Western territories because they did not want small farmers to have to compete with richer farmers who could afford the free labor of slaves.

freelance: a person who hires out his services independently without working under the control of one boss.

fugitive: someone who runs away to avoid being captured.

gag rule: a law that prevents people from talking about a specific subject.

gourd: a plant with a hard shell that is related to cucumbers and melons, but is not edible.

grassroots: an organization made up of many ordinary people.

hallucination: seeing, hearing, or smelling something that seems real but is usually caused by illness or a drug.

haven: a place where a person is protected from danger.

heroine: a woman admired for bravery.

hijack: to steal or kidnap.

hostility: great anger or strong dislike.

human trafficker: a person who illegally buys and sells people for the purpose of forcing them to work or to sexually abuse them.

ideal: a standard or belief that people strive to achieve.

illiterate: being unable to read or write.

immigrant: a person who settles in a new country.

immortalize: to be remembered forever.

imposter: a person pretending to be someone else.

incentive: something that encourages someone to do something.

indentured servant: a person bound by contract to work a certain number of years without pay.

influential: having power to make changes.

infusion: to introduce a new quality or custom into something.

inherited trait: a characteristic passed down from parent to child.

justify: to prove or show evidence that something is right.

Ku Klux Klan: a terrorist group formed after the Civil War that believed white Christians should hold the power in society.

legend: a story from the past that cannot be proved true.

literacy: the ability to read and write.

loophole: an error in a law that makes it possible for some people to legally disobey it.

metaphor: a figure of speech in which a word is used to symbolize another word.

Middle Passage: the forced voyage of enslaved Africans across the Atlantic Ocean to the Americas.

migrate: to move from one area to another.

minority: less than half of the population of a country.

monitor: to watch or keep track of something or someone.

morally: from the point of view of right and wrong action or good and bad character.

navigate: to find a way to get to a place when you are traveling.

network: a group of people who work together for a common cause.

oppression: an unjust or cruel use of authority and power.

orally: spoken.

overseer: a person who supervises workers.

patrol: people who systematically checked different areas in search of runaway slaves.

patroller: a person who walks around an area to make sure rules are being obeyed.

plague: to cause serious problems or irritation.

plantation: a large farm where one kind of crop is grown for export.

posse: a group gathered together by the sheriff to pursue a criminal.

poverty: to be poor.

predictable: to know what will happen next.

prostitution: to have sex in exchange for money.

province: a division of a country, similar to a state.

race: a group of people that shares distinct physical qualities, such as skin color.

racism: negative opinions or treatment of people based on race.

radical: someone who wants major change in social, political, or economic systems.

ransack: to search for something in a way that messes up or damages the place being searched.

ratify: to give official approval of something, such as a constitutional amendment.

rations: the food allowance for one day.

rebel: to resist authority.

rebellion: violent resistance to authority.

Reconstruction: the period of time after the Civil War when the United States was reorganized and reunited.

resistance: to fight to prevent something from happening.

reunite: to bring people together again after they have been apart for a long time.

revival: when something becomes popular after a long time of not being popular.

schooner: a sailing ship with two masts.

secede: to formally withdraw from a country.

segregate: to separate people based on race, religion, ethnicity, or some other category.

sinfulness: evil.

skiff: a shallow, flat-bottomed, open boat.

skimp: to give someone a very small amount of something.

slavery: when slaves are used as workers. A slave is a person owned by another person and forced to work, without pay, against their will.

slum: a crowded area of a city where poor people live and buildings are in bad condition.

sparse: few and scattered thinly over a wide area.

status: the position or rank of one group in society compared to another group.

stronghold: an area where most people have the same beliefs and values.

tarred and feathered: a form of mob punishment where pine tar, a thick, sticky substance, is heated and poured over a person, after which the individual is covered in feathers.

technology: tools, methods, and systems used to solve a problem or do work.

transatlantic slave trade: the buying and selling of enslaved Africans to buyers in Europe and the Americas that lasted from the fifteenth through the nineteenth centuries.

treason: the crime of betraying one's country.

trek: to walk for a long distance.

Triangular Trade: a transatlantic trade network in which slaves and manufactured goods were exchanged between Africa, Europe, the Caribbean, and the American colonies.

Underground Railroad: a system of cooperation among people who believed slavery was wrong that secretly helped fugitive slaves reach the Northern states and Canada.

unscrupulous: dishonest.

urgency: needing immediate attention.

verdict: a legal decision made by a judge or jury.

vocational: related to skills or training needed for a specific job.

warrant: a document issued by a court that gives the police the power to do something, such as search a building or arrest a person.

white supremacy: the racist belief that white people are superior to those of all other races, especially the black race, and should therefore dominate society.

with a vengeance: to an excessive or surprising degree.

BOOKS

Ayres, Katherine. *North by Night: A Story of the Underground Railroad.* Yearling, 2000.

Hansen, Joyce and Gary McGowan. *Freedom Roads: Searching for the Underground Railroad.* Cricket Books, 2003.

Lester, Julius. *Day of Tears.* Hyperion, 2007.

McKissack, Patricia. *Never Forgotten.* Schwartz & Wade, 2011.

Russell, Krista. *The Other Side of Free.* Peachtree, 2013.

Woodruff, Elvira. *Dear Austin: Letters from the Underground Railroad.* Yearling, 1998.

WEBSITES

The Underground Railroad: Escape from Slavery
teacher.scholastic.com/activities/bhistory/underground_railroad/

The Transatlantic Slave Trade
inmotionaame.org/migrations/landing.cfm;jsessionid=f8302
175081479898058807?migration=1&bhcp=1

Africans in American
pbs.org/wgbh/aia/home.html

Pathways to Freedom: Maryland and the Underground Railroad
pathways.thinkport.org/about

PLACES TO VISIT

Levi Coffin House (Fountain City, IN)
nps.gov/nr/travel/underground/in2.htm

Uncle Tom's Cabin (Dresden, ON)
www.uncletomscabin.org/homepg.htm

John P. Parker House (Ripley, OH)
ripleyohio.net/htm/oldpages/parker.htm

John Rankin House (Ripley, OH)
ripleyohio.net/htm/rankin.htm

National Underground Railroad Freedom Center (Cincinnati, OH)
freedomcenter.org

Milton House Museum (Milton, WI)
miltonhouse.org

ESSENTIAL QUESTIONS

Introduction: Why are there many myths and legends about the Underground Railroad?

Chapter 1: How did the U.S. Constitution enable Southern states to maintain the institution of slavery?

Chapter 2: What are some of the ways different groups of people objected to slavery before the Underground Railroad began?

Chapter 3: Why did the Underground Railroad start when it did? Why not sooner?

Chapter 4: What obstacles did fugitive slaves face in making their way to freedom and how did they overcome these obstacles?

Chapter 5: Why would slaves risk the dangers of escape to gain their freedom?

Chapter 6: Why did people help runaway slaves if it was so dangerous?

Chapter 7: Could slavery have been abolished without the Civil War?

Chapter 8: How has your daily life been influenced by the Underground Railroad?

RESOURCES

QR CODE GLOSSARY

Page 10: liverpoolmuseums.org.uk/ism/slavery/slave-stories/index.aspx

Page 12: newsdesk.si.edu/releases/national-museum-african-american-history-and-culture-display-objects-slave-shipwreck-found-

Page 16: learner.org/series/biographyofamerica/prog10/feature/index.html

Page 20: fullbooks.com/American-Cookery.html

Page 22: nmaahc.si.edu/explore/collection/search?edan_q=%2A%3A%2A&edan_local=1&edan_q%5B%5D=topic%3A%22Slavery%22

Page 25: pbs.org/independentlens/natturner/slave_rebellions.html#1838

Page 32: slavevoyages.org/voyage/search

Page 54: eduplace.com/kids/socsci/books/applications/imaps/maps/g5s_u6

Page 61: youtube.com/watch?v=pw6N_eTZP2U

Page 84: deila.dickinson.edu/cdm/ref/collection/ownwords/id/47570

Page 91: archive.org/details/undergroundrailr00stil

Page 91: digitalcollections.nypl.org/items/510d47db-bccb-a3d9-e040-e00a18064a99

Page 112: endslaverynow.org/learn/slavery-today

INDEX